ASTROLOGY
NUTRITION
& HEALTH

BY ROBERT CARL JANSKY

A Division of Schiffer Publishing
4880 Lower Valley Rd.
Atglen, PA 19310 USA

84-

Astrology, Nutrition & Health
by Robert Carl Jansky

ISBN: 978-0-914918-08-0
Printed in China

Schiffer Books are available at special discounts for bulk purchases for sales
promotions or premiums. Special editions, including personalized covers,
corporate imprints, and excerpts can be created in large quantities for special
needs. For more information contact the publisher:

Published by Schiffer Publishing Ltd.
4880 Lower Valley Road
Atglen, PA 19310
Phone: (610) 593-1777; Fax: (610) 593-2002
E-mail: Info@schifferbooks.com

For the largest selection of fine reference books on this and related subjects,
please visit our web site at: **www.schifferbooks.com**
We are always looking for people to write books on new and related subjects.
If you have an idea for a book please contact us at the above address.

This book may be purchased from the publisher.
Include $5.00 for shipping.
Please try your bookstore first.
You may write for a free catalog.

In Europe, Schiffer books are distributed by
Bushwood Books
6 Marksbury Ave.
Kew Gardens
Surrey TW9 4JF England
Phone: 44 (0) 20 8392 8585; Fax: 44 (0) 20 8392 9876
E-mail: info@bushwoodbooks.co.uk
Website: www.bushwoodbooks.co.uk

CONTENTS

FOREWORD

Can your health problems be identified through an analysis of particular factors in your natal horoscope? By taking proper preventative measures, can these problems be minimized or avoided? In this unprecedented book, Robert Jansky attempts to answer questions such as these, introducing the reader to a fascinating and productive area of modern astrological research.

Astrology, which can be considered the most ancient art and science, has always been concerned with the interplay of energy between the macrocosm and the microcosm--between the universe and the individual. Both macrocosm and microcosm are composed of shining orbs whirling in intelligent orderly motion. The universe is made up of moons, planets, atoms and molecules. In the cosmos, there are cosmic rays, ribbons of intelligent energy that guide, renew and integrate these multiple parts into a single whole. Likewise, electromagnetic emanations from the nucleus of the atom and its electrons integrate the whole physical body as one purposeful working, living unit.

This cohesive universal order should be obvious to anyone who has observed the movements of the stars or watched the germination of a plant or witnessed the birth of a baby. Although astrology is much older than the sciences of medicine, chiropractic or nutrition, this ancient and revealing body of knowledge has been overlooked by almost all scientists, nutritionists and healing arts practitioners. Because astrology is empirical, based on gross observation and unproved in the test tube or under the microscope, it is generally considered irrelevant to scientific studies. The scientific world of the twentieth century has become so overly analytical and specialized that it cannot easily embrace wholistic concepts that reveal the interdependence of life and nature on all levels.

It was Hippocrates, the father of healing, who wrote that one could not do a thorough job of healing the sick without a basic knowledge of astrological principles. He also strongly emphasized the healing power of nature, the natural recuperative power of the body and the importance of the spine. Yet almost no one in the healing arts has utilized the diagnostic tools and preventive health measures available to those who understand the astrological principles explained in this book.

Astrology, Nutrition and Health responds to a present need and an ancient call, for it studies the relationship between the astrological symbolism in an individual's natal chart and what happens biochemically and physiologically in his or her body. Jansky is keenly interested here in explaining the fundamental techniques needed to carry on this branch of research. He clarifies his teachings with relevant examples gathered over many years of experience as a professional astrologer, enlarged by his expertise in biochemistry. Several chapters are devoted to the roles and astrological significance of proteins, carbohydrates, enzymes, hormones, vitamins, minerals and cell salts in nutrition. Do you realize that if you were born in January you may require more calcium than does someone who was born in July? Studies confirming this kind of astrological theory could add important knowledge to the field of preventative health care. We must not overlook any tool that can alleviate disease or pain and save lives!

This book does not pretend to be a substitute for necessary professional health care nor a complete work from which students might practice on others. Much research is needed in this field, and it takes considerable practice and experience for anyone to become really adept in this branch of

astrology. Therefore, Jansky cautions the reader against draw-
ing any hasty conclusions from his or her own or another
person's natal chart.

The principal concern of this book is learning how to
maintain good health, which is also the concern of the nutritionist, the chiropractor and others who are turning their attention toward preventive health care and away from drugs and
crisis therapy. Astrology is concerned with anticipating events
in our lives before they occur, and astrological research seems to
show that health and nutritional problems can be anticipated.
To be forewarned is to be forearmed.

Since *Astrology, Nutrition and Health* is the first book of
its kind, it is a stepping stone to more study and further
breakthroughs in this field. Hopefully this material will be
evaluated objectively by other researchers in the healing arts,
perhaps with the aid of computers. I believe Hippocrates would
have wanted it that way.

Bruce Eric Hedendal, D.C.
Doctor of Chiropractic,
Columbia College of Chiropractic
President, Wholistic Health Foundation

INTRODUCTION

Once upon a time in a distant kingdom, it happened that after the grain crop had been harvested and stored, it was discovered to be poisoned. Anyone who ate it went insane. The King and his advisors immediately took counsel as to what should be done. Clearly, not enough food was available from other sources to sustain the population. There was no choice but to eat the grain. Very well, the King said, let us eat it. But at the same time we must feed a few people on a different diet so there will be among us some who remember we are insane.

Newsweek, January 13, 1975

Our Creator has given each of us the right to choose freely the materials that we incorporate into our bodies, our minds and ultimately our souls. However, you must remember that whatever you incorporate into yourself ultimately becomes an integral part of you. The food you eat, the thoughts you think eventually become *you*.

In the New Testament of the Bible, in the ninth chapter of Luke is the parable of feeding the multitudes with five loaves of bread and two fishes. Those who know the rich and beautiful symbolism of astrology will immediately recognize the correspondence between this parable and the symbolism of Virgo,

1

representing the grain of wheat, and its opposite sign Pisces, which represents the fishes. Virgo symbolizes food from plant sources; Pisces, food from the animal kingdom. In the horoscope these two signs are the natural rulers of the sixth and the twelfth house, which deal with the health and sustenance of the physical body.

In another sense, Virgo represents whatever is real, tangible, physical in form and structure and capable of analysis. Pisces, on the other hand, represents the nontangible, the unreal, those elements of life that cannot be easily analyzed because they are nonphysical and otherworldly. In this sense, Virgo–Pisces represents the spectrum of kinds of food that we choose to incorporate into our bodies. Each of us is free to choose, either consciously or by instinct, where in this broad spectrum we shall place ourselves. Mercury, ruler of Virgo and of conscious thought, symbolizes a planned approach to basic nutrition. Neptune, ruler of Pisces, represents the unconscious element in our choices. Some choices we make rationally and consciously, others we make merely because we feel like it, for no particular reason.

If you have chosen to be a vegetarian, a fruitarian, a natural food advocate, you have chosen a place in this spectrum close to Mercury and Virgo. If you choose your food according to what you feel like eating at the moment or according to what an expert has told you, your position is closer to the Pisces end. Those at the Virgo extreme eat nothing but natural foods, unpolluted by artificial additives and almost wholly vegetable. Those at the Pisces extreme accept all unnatural food additives, select foods by pure instinct with no thought for their nutritional content and eat a high proportion of animal or meat products.

All of us, by conscious thought or simply by habit, are at some point between these two extremes. But as thinking human beings, we are free to choose our point in the spectrum and free to change it as we learn and study more about astrology and nutrition. One purpose of this book is to help you select your position in this spectrum more wisely. I do not believe that either extreme is tenable for long. A totally vegetarian or fruitarian diet deprives the body of essential nutrients that can be obtained in sufficient quantity only from animal sources or by artificial means, both of which are ruled by Neptune. On the other hand, it is just as dangerous to load the body with artificial substances or to select foods on the advice of so-called experts without question.

Where then is the happy solution, the middle ground? That can be found only through learning and knowledge, for which there is no substitute. Free will is not enough. Free will requires intelligent choices based on education, represented by the third house of the horoscope, and through personal experience and wisdom gained in the process of living, represented by the ninth house.

Unlike the kingdom in the parable I quoted, our food source has not yet been poisoned. It is not yet necessary to select a "privileged few" who will remind us that we are insane. Remember, Christ fed the multitudes with *both* bread and fishes, Virgo *and* Pisces.

Astrology teaches us the importance of being in balance (Libra) with our external environment. Through Scorpio we learn to separate the beneficial elements from the waste, which is then eliminated. Only then can we hope to achieve growth and expansion—the promise of Sagittarius.

The more you know about what you are doing to your body when you put various foods into your system, the more intelligent you can be in selecting your place in the Virgo-Pisces spectrum. Understanding the basic symbolism and meaning of your natal horoscope can help you make this choice more wisely. Astrology, the healing arts and nutrition all have developed historically from our need to understand the influences on our lives. In writing this book, my purposes have been to clarify the connection among these three important areas of study, to retrace the steps that have brought us where we are today and to suggest some paths for future research.

1

THE ORIGINS
OF MEDICAL ASTROLOGY

To the average person who reads the astrology column in the daily newspaper, the statement that those "fun predictions" have some serious relationship to their health would probably be startling, if not ludicrous. To serious pracitioners of the medical arts, such a statement borders on heresy! Nevertheless, a serious study of the foundations of medical practice would demonstrate that medicine developed from astrology. Astrology begat medicine (as well as most of the other modern sciences, either directly or indirectly) and in turn, medicine begat nutrition. Each of these sciences is concerned with maintaining good health, which is the principal concern of this book.

Astrology in Ancient Times

Astrology goes back several millenia to the rich alluvial plains of Chaldea, which lie between the mighty Tigris and Euphrates rivers. According to present-day research, the ancient people who lived here—the Chaldeans—were principally shepherds. It was a wild land, where jackals and other predators roved, waiting to pounce upon a stray sheep. Thus, the shepherds had to remain vigilant against attack night and day. The land, originally covered by the sea, is a vast and almost perfectly flat plain. With no mountains and few clouds to obstruct their view of the heavens, it is natural that the shepherds turned their attention to the firmament and studied the movements of the stars and planets.

As a child, perhaps you had books in which you connected a series of numbered dots to make a picture. That is what the Chaldeans did mentally with the stars, making pictures of their gods and of familiar animals in their environment: the ram, Aries; the bull, Taurus; the bear, Ursa; the dog, Canis; the lion, Leo; and so on.

Under such ideal viewing conditions, the sky must have been a fascinating and awe-inspiring sight. The nightly movement of the starry configurations, which changed as the year progressed, helped the Chaldeans to time, and thus predict, the seasonal changes that occurred on earth. Thus, it was natural to postulate some sort of correspondence between celestial phenomena and terrestrial events.

The stars formed a kind of backdrop against which certain lights, principally the Moon, seemed to travel in a predictable path. When these wandering stars (the planets) entered certain constellations, the Chaldeans noted correspondences to natural phenomena on the earth. The Moon's movement, of course, was their first concern, but other wandering stars—Mercury, Venus, Mars, Jupiter and Saturn—later drew their attention.

Later, the Babylonians released certain people, whom they called priests, from the mundane task of herding in order to devote all their time to studying the heavens and the portent of the stars. Jupiter, which the ancient Babylonians called Marduk, was their most important deity. Marduk was at first the principal god of battle and later the "restorer of happiness and joy" to the afflicted. Thus Marduk (Jupiter) today has become the principal symbol of all who heal, of wisdom and knowledge, of the guru, the priest, the expert.

Every civilization that modern man has studied places the healer, or medicine man, symbolized by Jupiter, only slightly lower in rank than the chieftain of the tribe or nation, who is usually symbolized by the Sun. For many centuries, the secret knowledge of these medicine men or priests was feared by tribal members who did not possess their "occult" knowledge. In modern society, until very recently, the doctor was similarly revered by the public as being only a little less than God. Jupiter, along with its natural sign, Sagittarius, and its natural house, the ninth, thus became associated with higher wisdom and learning, religious belief, the occult and the esoteric.

The Chaldeans and the Babylonians associated the meanings of astrology with the fate of nations and tribes and their leaders. It was left to the later Greek observers to personalize astrology for the individual. It may have been the Greek astronomer Anaximander, around 600 B.C., who first thought of the earth as spherical rather than flat. Nearly a hundred years later, Pythagoras elaborated this idea and founded a new system of mathematics, a necessary tool to understanding celestial movements. He also established the science of numerology, which some scholars consider the forerunner of modern astrology. The Greek philosopher Plato, along with Aristarchus of Samos and Eudoxus of Cnidus, recognized that the planets varied in their distance and speed as they moved around the Sun. Eratosthenes, who followed them, was the first to estimate the earth's circumference. Hipparchus first recognized the cyclic nature of the heavenly bodies in relation to earthly events, and upon his observations was based the monumental work of the astronomer Ptolemy who, in essence, formulated much of our modern astrological theory. Ptolemy's *Tetrabiblos* records the structure of Greek astrology as well as ancient medical practice.

Using Ptolemy's system of correspondences, Hippocrates, the father of modern medicine, built his philosophical system. Today every new doctor must swear to uphold the code of medical ethics known as the Hippocratic oath. And it was the great Hippocrates himself who reminded all practitioners of the medical arts that no one could do an adequate job of healing the sick without a basic knowledge of astrological principles. Hippocrates had discovered what most modern practitioners have forgotten or overlooked: that astrology can make an important contribution to the healing process as well as to maintenance of good physical health

However, before we get too carried away by the importance of astrology to the medical profession, let's try to keep it in proper perspective. The ancient sages never considered astrology as a replacement for medical procedures. At its highest and best, astrology is only a *diagnostic tool,* to be used by the doctor as only one of many important tools and tests in the diagnosis and prognosis of disease conditions. However, the importance of astrology as a diagnostic tool in the doctor's "bag of tricks" has been sadly underrated and needs to be given much more emphasis by present-day medical practitioners.

To ask someone, "Do you believe in astrology?" is as ridiculous as asking, "Do you believe in medicine or chemistry or biology or weather forecasting?" Like the other systematized bodies of knowledge, astrology *is!* It does not require "belief," for it is as much a science as any of the other so-called sciences. And when we apply its teachings to the improvement of life, it becomes an art just like medicine or weather forecasting. The facts remain the facts—it is simply how we *interpret* them that is the issue. And different people interpret facts differently.

Astrology can be put to many uses. For example, certain groups have chosen to incorporate the teachings of astrology into their particular brand of religious belief. However, this does not make astrology "star worship." To call astrology star worship because certain people give a metaphysical interpretation to the natal chart would be like calling meteorology "weather worship" because the American Indians chose to worship a rain god or the Incas a sun god. Zoology is not "animal worship" just because certain primitive cultures chose to worship the bull as sacred, because the Indians hold the cow sacred or because Christians worship Jesus as the "lamb of God!"

I believe that astrology is used for the greatest good when it is considered as one set of basic symbols (not unlike our alphabet) to better understand and express our relationship to our environment. In the hands of the astrologer-psychologist, it can be a most valuable tool in helping us understand our own behavior and how this behavior manifests from time to time in the symptoms of disease. It can help us understand why we think and act as we do. On the other hand, astrology has been used in divining the future, which is often merely fortune-telling, and this has contributed largely to its disrepute. In fact, the practice of astrology is illegal in many municipalities, for what man fears, he attempts to protect himself from, and those who can forecast the future are feared.

Modern Medicine and Nutrition

Astrology has been on the scene for over 4,000 years; modern medical practice had its origin less than 100 years ago; and nutrition is barely 50 years old. Most authorities consider Louis Pasteur to be the father of modern medicine, because of his important discoveries. Before Pasteur's time, most Church authorities thought it heresy to apply chemistry and biology to the human condition. Primitive attempts had been made to understand the chemistry of urine, and the presence of sugar in the urine had been recognized as a symptom of diabetes for many years, but no one who wanted to keep his head on his shoulders dared suggest seriously that the laws of nature and chemistry applied to the human being, cast in God's own image.

In Pasteur's time in the late 1800's, chemistry was a new science. Hundreds of chemical reactions take place in every individual living cell, but scientists had no way of studying chemical reactions on this minute scale or even realizing that they existed. The role of minerals in the diet was unknown, and vitamins had not been discovered. In the early 1600's Harvey had discovered that blood circulates within the body, but the fact that outside agents like bacteria, protozoa and viruses could cause disease was not known. Plague, tuberculosis and smallpox were rampant. In the migration to the West in the United States, thousands died from diphtheria. Surgery was still performed by barbers. Even as late as the early 1900's, astrology books stated that the spinal canal contained "humours" or gaseous substances that liquefied only when penetrated by a hypodermic needle.

What was required was a sophisticated method for studying minute chemical reactions in the body, which had to wait for the development of modern electronic technology in the 1940's. However, some excellent pioneering work was done before that time by scientists who attempted to wed the sciences of biology and chemistry into a new field of research called "biochemistry." Pasteur was perhaps the first true biochemist.

For the most part, modern American medical practice may be described as *allopathic* medicine—a system that combats disease by administering chemical remedies (drugs) to counteract the symptoms of the disease. In general, these drugs are artificial chemicals that are not part of a healthy person's diet, and although they alleviate the symptoms of the disease, they do not go to the heart of the problem. Instead, they block some natural body process or function. The few exceptions to this are the antibiotics and such natural substances as thyroxin (thyroid extract) and insulin, all of which have a natural origin.

Modern medical practice is actually in its infancy, for far less is known about the basic chemistry and functioning of the body than most people imagine. Billions of aspirin tablets are sold each year for the relief of minor pain, and yet no medical doctor can adequately explain in simple terms why aspirin relieves pain. Modern medicine simply does not yet know how aspirin works! Most of our modern drugs are used because, on the basis of empirical observation, they relieve the symptoms of disease without causing undesirable side effects in most people.

Although aspirin is now synthesized in the laboratory, it was originally extracted from the bark of the willow tree. In fact, until the 1930's, most of the so-called drugs in the doctor's satchel were extracted from natural plant substances. Quinine, from the South American cinchona tree, was used for the relief of fever and malarial symptoms. Digitalis, from the foxglove plant, relieved circulatory problems. Belladonna, a species of nightshade, was used to treat nausea and vomiting. Licorice and cascara were laxatives, and ipecac was the emetic used to induce vomiting. Molasses, from sugar cane, was mixed with naturally occurring sulfur and taken as a general tonic. Crude horse serums were used in the treatment of such diseases as pneumonia. For centuries, alcohol, distilled from natural grains and fruits, was the only anesthetic and disinfectant. It was not until the late 1800's that chloroform and then ether became available as general anesthetics in surgery, and nitrous oxide (laughing gas) in dental procedures. During World War II the discovery of the synthetic sulfa drugs saved the lives of thousands of wounded soldiers. And later, penicillin, which was originally derived from *Penicillium notatum*, a simple mold, proved such a great boon to combating infection.

Today, the South American Indians think us civilized people "crazy" in our inordinate hunger for chocolate, a substance that they use only as a drug. The rauwolfia plant, from which we extract an essential alkaloid, is used in the treatment of high blood pressure. And the list of natural medicines goes on and on. Even marijuana is beginning to find medicinal use in relieving fluid pressure within the eyeball caused by glaucoma, as well as in treating asthma.

Scientific Evidence of Astrology

THE TAKATA EXPERIMENTS. In 1938, Dr. Maki Takata at Toho University in Japan began a biochemical study of the ovarian cycle in the human female. The presence of chemical messengers, called "hormones," in the body had only recently been recognized, and their monumental influence on personality and physical development was not yet understood.

To carry out his program of research, Takata needed to develop a method of removing the protein albumin from the blood, because this substance interfered with his work. Takata's method, now called the Takata reaction, consists of adding certain compounds to a blood sample, causing the albumin to flocculate or precipitate out of the liquid portion of the blood so that it can then be removed by centrifuging.

Up until this time, scientists had believed it to be an ironclad law that if a series of identical chemical reactions was performed under the same set of conditions (heat, light, purity, humidity, etc.) each reaction would proceed at the same rate in any geographical location. Takata discovered that this law did not seem to apply to his albumin flocculation reaction. At certain times it went faster, at other times slower. He set out to discover why this was so, after carefully verifying that other scientists using his test around the world were observing a similar phenomenon.

Takata assumed that this variation in rate for the precipitation of albumin in the blood did not occur in males. But in January, 1938, he observed this phenomenon in the blood of males as well! Takata was determined to discover the cause of this cyclical variation in the precipitation mechanism. After examining all plausible explanations, none of which corresponded to his findings, he was driven to examine the implausible causes; it turned out that the rate of the reaction varied with the time of day, the date of the year, the eleven-year sunspot cycle, eclipses and magnetic storms in the earth's ionosphere. Heresy! Clearly, celestial influences were exerting a powerful influence upon the protein in the blood. Takata knew that proteins are the only chemical substances capable of "life" as we know it on earth, and here he had demonstrated in his test tubes that celestial influences were affecting the chemical behavior of this protein. Could they be affecting the other proteins in the body as well?

Proteins belong to a group of substances known to chemists as colloids. In 1951, at the University of Florence in Italy, Dr. Giorgio Piccardi became interested in Takata's work and decided to repeat the Takata experiments, this time using a nonbiological colloid called oxychloral bismuth, which is prepared by dissolving trichloral bismuth in water. Heresy upon heresy—Piccardi discovered that the speed of this oxychloral bismuth reaction also varied according to celestial conditions! Unusual sunspot activity, eclipses and magnetic storms tended to interfere with and slow down the reaction, while periods of lesser cosmic activity tended to speed it up.

In 1954, Caroli and Pichotka in Germany took the work of Takata and Piccardi and demonstrated again that the rate of reaction varied with time and celestial conditions. There seemed little doubt that something out there in the heavens was definitely affecting events on the earth. They could see it with their own eyes and time it with their stopwatches.

Piccardi also made another fascinating discovery when a boiler technician at the university complained to him that twice each year the rust in his boilers peeled off and contaminated the water. And he could do nothing to control it. Piccardi theorized that the surface tension of the boiler water must have been reduced for some unexplained reason. But why? He noted that this phenomenon always occurred in September and March (to the astrologer, when the Sun is transiting through Virgo and Pisces). When the surface tension of water is reduced, it becomes "wetter." Softening agents added to wash water reduce the surface tension, thus increasing the water's ability to dissolve dirt. In Piccardi's case, the softened water even dissolved the rust.

Schwenk's experiments seem to support the idea of moving rapidly under favorable cosmic influences and more slowly when the influences are adverse, for by remaining relatively quiet we are far less susceptible to outside influences. That, of course, is the purpose of bed rest after an illness.

BIOLOGICAL CLOCKS. At Northwestern University Dr. Frank Brown has done some fascinating work on a mechanism that seems to be built into all living things, which Brown calls biological clocks. This refers to the ability of a living organism to sense changes in the Earth's magnetic field, which is only one ten-millionth as strong as the emanations given off in the immediate area of home electrical appliances. These changes in the Earth's magnetic field follow a predictable schedule related to the positions of the Sun, Moon and planets. For example, Brown discovered that oysters kept their cycle of opening and closing according to the Moon-timed tidal phase of their original home even when transported a thousand miles inland.

This biological clock mechanism can eaily be tested in

your own home. In the fall, place some flower bulbs in the darkest part of your cellar, away from all light, and leave them there until the following spring. Check them periodically, and you will find that they do not sprout during the winter months. But when their normal growing time arrives in spring, they will sprout even in storage.

When bulbs are stored, the tissues do not die, they "breathe." Dr. Brown carefully measured the rate of respiration (utilization of oxygen) by bulbs in the stored condition. His experiments showed that as spring approaches, the rate of respiration increases; they require and use more oxygen. The only possible signal these bulbs could receive is from the magnetic-cosmic field surrounding the Earth.

If you wish to learn more about biological clocks, read *The Living Clocks*, by Ritchie R. Ward, published by Alfred A. Knopf, New York. It contains a very fascinating account of this research.

RADIO TRANSMISSION. Perhaps some of the strongest supportive evidence for astrology, especially the effect of aspects, has come from another non-astrologer, John H. Nelson of RCA. In the earlier days of long-distance (short-wave) radio, it was observed that ionospheric conditions had a marked effect upon the quality of short-wave broadcasting. It was important to RCA to be able to predict in advance when transmitting conditions would be adverse so that arrangements could be made to bypass the interference.

They awarded grants totaling several million dollars to some astronomers, who spent the money but produced little of value. RCA then turned to their own engineering staff, headed by John Nelson, who discovered that he could predict the conditions of transmission quite accurately by looking at the angular relationship between the planets on a given day: in other words, planetary aspects.

His forecasts were more than 95 percent accurate, according to the U.S. Department of Commerce in numerous yearly publications. Nelson describes his work in the book *Cosmic Pat-*

terns—Their Influence on Man and His Communication, published by the American Federation of Astrologers.

At about the same time, Bell Laboratories in New Jersey was also interested in this phenomenon, because the telephone network sends its signals by microwaves, which are very sensitive radio waves transmitted from tower to tower along a line of sight. Atmospheric conditions garbled these transmissions too. Bell Labs assigned this problem to Dr. Karl Jansky, who developed an electronic receiving instrument called a parabolic reflector, with which he was able to focus on certain sectors of the heavens and "zero" in on interfering radio-wave sources of radio transmission in the heavens where no stars could be found by even the most powerful telescopes.

Jansky's findings led to the brand-new field of radio astronomy, which specializes in locating stars that radiate radio waves but no visible light. Jansky subsequently became known as the "father of radio astronomy" and his invention, the parabolic reflector, was the prototype of radar transmitting and receiving equipment.

THE HUMAN AURA. For many years certain individuals have claimed the ability to see "auras," that is, colors radiated by certain forms of energy in the body. Science at first gave this little credence, but within the last few years, specialized techniques have made it possible to actually photograph auras. The leaders in this field have been Russian researchers and scientists of the University of California at Los Angeles, notably Dr. Thelma Moss.

Physicists have long known that when current flows through a conducting material, such as an electrical wire, it sets up an electromagnetic field about the conductor. This current can be measured by an electrical instrument called a galvanometer, which is the principle on which electrical generators are based.

The human nervous system is also a conductor of electrical current. Messages are transmitted over the nerve fibers via tiny electrical impulses that can be measured with such instruments as the electrocardiograph and electroencephalograph. (Alpha and beta brain waves are electrical waves.) We already know that when current moves through a conductor, it sets up a magnetic field around the conductor, and this magnetic field is probably the "aura" that certain people claim to see.

When the drum or armature of a generator moves within a magnetic field, or cuts magnetic lines of force, it creates a flow of energy. Likewise, as your body moves, cutting the lines of magnetic force flowing from the Earth's magnetic poles, a counter current is set up along the conducting fibers of the nervous system. Thus, we can clearly see from the preceding experiments that the galactic cosmic field influences the earth's magnetic field, and that changes in the earth's magnetic field influence the electrical character of the transmissions of the nervous sytem. Thus, a cause and effect relationship can be established "scientifically" between what is going on "out there"and what is happening here on Earth.

ADDEY'S RESEARCH. Astrologers have not been totally "out of it" all this time. We just haven't had the means to communicate our findings through scholarly journals as scientists do. One British astrologer, John Addey, has made another breakthrough. His mathematical and statistical work links astrology with nuclear physics rather directly. Addey took the birth times of more than 7,000 medical doctors and clergymen and computer-sorted them according to the location of the Sun in space at the moment of birth. Addey found that many of the doctors' birthdates were grouped every one-fifth, twenty-fifth and one hundred twenty-fifth of the way along the circle of the zodiac signs, beginning at the vernal point of 0° Aries (where many of the birthtimes he studied were clumped).

Why did the number five figure so importantly? According to classical numerology, five is the natural number of the healer. Paracelsus, father of modern pharmacology (the science that deals with drugs), wrote of the correspondence of fiveness with healing. Addey rediscovered this phenomenon, as any modern statistician would, when he subjected the data to harmonic analysis (Fourier analysis). This was exactly the method used by such renowned nuclear scientists as deBroglie in the 1930's to unlock the secrets of the atom.

Addey also showed that the birthtimes of clergymen tended to be grouped about sevenths and forty-ninths of the zodiac circle. The number seven, which is mentioned many times in the Bible, is the number most closely associated with mystical religious symbolism.

Much more research is being carried out today, primarily in England and France. One of the most comprehensive studies was done by the French astrologer Gauquelin, who studied and categorized thousands of birthdates according to profession. Gauquelin's initial objective in this research was to disprove astrology, but the results of his research have made him a believer.

The scientific proofs for astrology continue to multiply. However, as scientific knowledge proliferates, scientists must become more and more specialized, to the point that research in one area goes unnoticed by a scientist in a different area who might profit by it. Sadly, this is exactly what has happened in astrology, principally because it has never been accepted as a legitimate science, despite the experimental evidence we have just described, and also because astrological research has never been adequately funded.

Pharmacology and Nutrition

Pharmacology is concerned with the physiological effect of "foreign" substances introduced into the body: in other words, drugs and poisons. How or why the early drugs worked was not of particular concern to doctors at that time. The fact that they worked at all was the important thing. The ancients and not-so-ancients had discovered the curative properties of certain herbs, and that was that.

But there were those who "cared." And these pharmacologists and herbalists set out to discover why certain drugs worked and how they changed the chemistry of the body. Some biochemists who related the first biochemical discoveries to diet in order to improve the health of the body were in fact nutritionists. The discovery in this century of certain chemical compounds essential to body health, called vitamins, spurred this research on.

Unfortunately, both biochemists and nutritionists overlooked a vast body of knowledge, which at the time was in disrepute, that would have helped them immeasurably. That body of knowledge, of course, was astrology, the oldest science. Because astrology is empirical, based upon gross observation alone and unprovable in the test tube or under the microscope, it was generally considered irrelevant to their studies. This situation is still not much changed today, but the nutritionists are learning, as are the forward-looking astrologers. One day the teachings of all three sciences will be merged for the greater benefit of mankind. Perhaps this book will help. It is the first attempt that I know of to bring together the teachings of medicine, nutrition and health.

Your Astro-Nutritional Library

A question that my students often ask is, "What books do you recommend that I buy for my astro-nutritional library?" A good library of this sort should contain not only books on medical astrology, and there are a very few on this subject, but also some good basic texts on anatomy, physiology and nutrition. In order to study and understand any health condition, it is necessary to first understand *in detail* how the diseased area of the body functions normally and then what has happened to this area because of the abnormal condition. It is also necessary to understand how the subject's nutritional habits and psychological factors may contribute to this condition.

Possibly the best basic textbook for the layman on anatomy and physiology that I have seen to date is *The Rand-McNally Atlas of the Body and Mind* edited by Mitchell

Beazley, published by Rand McNally, Chicago, 1976. It is beautifully illustrated, nontechnical in approach, and covers this entire field extremely well. This book is more expensive than most you will buy (over twenty dollars), but it is certainly worth the cost.

The foundation stone of your library should be the monumental treatise *Encyclopedia of Medical Astrology* by H. L. Cornell, M.D., now in its third revised edition, published jointly by Llewellyn Publications in St. Paul, Minnesota, and Samuel Weiser, Inc., in New York City. Cornell wrote this book in 1933, at a time when little was known about Pluto. The revised edition contains an introduction by Laurel Lowell with more recent findings regarding Pluto. In this book you can find the astrological symbolism corresponding to any medical problem that was recognized at the time Cornell wrote the book. Of course much that we now understand was not recognized in the 1930's, so you will not be able to find everything here that you might be looking for. However, this book is as complete as any that exists now and much more accurate than all of the others, in my opinion.

The book stores are full of books today on nutrition—some excellent and some bordering on quackery. About the best textbook I've found on this subject for the layman is *Nutrition Almanac*, written by Nutrition Search, Inc., John D. Kirschmann, director, and published in 1975 by McGraw-Hill Book Company. Within these pages is all of the information on nutrition you'll need. I am particularly impressed by the section on various disease conditions and the nutrients that may be beneficial in treating them. A considerable portion of the book is devoted to the nutritional content of the common foods we eat, information that is vital in planning a well-balanced diet.

You will wish to add many other books to your library, but the three mentioned above are the core; they should provide well over 90 percent of the information you seek.

2

BASIC TOOLS
OF MEDICAL ASTROLOGY

Can a person's potential health problems be identified through particular factors in the natal horoscope? With proper preventive measures, can such problems be minimized or avoided? The answer is unequivocally yes.

Recognizing that most astrologers are not trained healers and are not licensed to practice medicine, how should they answer a client's questions about health? The easy answer, of course, is that they should not concern themselves with health at all. An astrologer who admits to a lack of expertise in health matters is hardly discredited as an advisor in other areas. If anything, his image is enhanced, for an intelligent client will recognize that this person knows his limitations. Also this approach protects the astrologer from any accusations of practicing medicine without a license.

However, if this were your attitude, you probably would never have picked up this book. If I believed that an astrologer should ignore health problems, I would never have written this book, nor would I have gotten interested in astrology in the first place. The intriguing fact is, the horoscope can be used as a diagnostic tool for health purposes. By learning how to use this tool, an astrologer can give a client additional information, and all of us as individuals can have a better understanding of our health.

The old saw, "He who treats himself has a fool for a patient," certainly contains a kernel of truth, but it oversimplifies and obscures an even greater truth. An individual can do a great deal to anticipate potential health problems and lessen their effect, long before it is necessary to seek professional help. This is called preventive medicine, and the healing professions are taking that direction today. With adequate knowledge of the body's parts and their functions and with the right tools for recognizing potential problems (one such tool being an accurately timed natal chart), we can actually improve our health. Also, when we as astrologers spot a potential health problem in a client's chart, we can advise the client to seek professional attention for that problem. Thus the astrologer does not have to be considered as an adversary by doctors but as someone who assists the therapist in his major job, the prevention and treatment of disease.

In order for astrologers to fulfill this function, we must become familiar with the anatomy and physiology of the body as well as with the basic symbolism of medical astrology. But remember, unless you understand what a symbol represents, you can't understand the symbol. The letters c-o-w have no meaning unless you know what a cow is, and to say that Mars represents the adrenal glands is of no help unless the astrologer knows what these glands are as well as their bodily function.

Astrological Polarities

Like science, astrology has many theories but few laws. I am always amazed at the number of astrology students and even teachers who have never consciously come to grips with the fundamental law of astrological polarities. One can never hope to fully grasp the significance and meaning of signs and houses without understanding this law. It is especially important to an understanding of astrology in relation to nutrition and health.

Most astrologers have had the experience of someone saying, "I am an Aries. Tell me what that means." After hearing a description of some basic Aries characteristics, the person shakes his head and replies, "That doesn't describe me at all! I'm not very impulsive, I listen to other people's advice, and I'm not overconfident or egotistical. I try to consider others' feelings before I act, and I go out of my way to avoid a fight." Sounds more like a Libra than an Aries, doesn't he? The fact is, quite a number of people born with the Sun in Aries act more like Aries' opposite sign, Libra. If astrology has any relevance in describing an individual's personality, this seeming discrepancy must be explained. It is not enough to say that perhaps these people have their Moon or a stellium in Libra, because a great many of them have no Libra emphasis in the horoscope at all. Then what is the explanation?

Aries cannot be fully understood or properly interpreted without an understanding of its opposite number, Libra, just as good has no real meaning unless we understand bad, and black does not make sense without white. Each concept has its archetype and its opposite. The Christ represents "good" in its purest form, while Satan represents "bad" in the extreme. When we study the twelve signs in astrology, we learn about the archetype of each sign, realizing that few people will actually fit the archetype exactly. However, you cannot understand the exceptions until you fully understand the rule.

In America we have a passion for classifying everything and everybody, distrusting whatever can't be neatly classified as Democrat or Republican, Catholic or Jew, black or white, male or female. But such a classification system does not work, as we are beginning to see when we attempt to classify people by ethnic group to prevent job discrimination, or athletes as male or female when some have actually changed their sex, or couples who live together as married or single for legal purposes. We can set up archetypes, but we are really dealing with shades of gray, not black or white. And this applies just as much when we attempt to classify people astrologically.

In reality, when it comes to house and sign interpretation, we are dealing with a spectrum. If you were born on April 1, you were born when the Earth and the Sun were aligned in the

Aries-Libra axis or *polarity,* and thus your basic individuality incorporates characteristics of both signs. Every planet in your horoscope is not just "in" one sign. Its position, when considered as aligned with the Earth, is in a sign pair or polarity that embodies certain common characteristics of both signs. To become a competent astrologer, one must recognize this fundamental fact.

This brings us to the age-old philosophical-religious problem of free will. Does man control his life, or has everything been predetermined ahead of time by some master architect of the universe? As with all polar situations, neither extreme is correct. Man's will does play a role, but so does fate, and heredity is an important factor also. All the wishing in the world cannot turn a giant into a midget nor change the color of one's skin. Heredity establishes certain constants or limits within which each person must learn to live. Within these limits, however, each individual has considerable latitude as to how he or she will develop.

If you were born in the Aries-Libra spectrum, there is nothing you can do about that either. It is a constant. However, you have considerable latitude as to where in this spectrum you choose to place yourself at any given moment. The diagram below illustrates this.

The brackets represent the extremes of the Aries-Libra polarity. A child with his natal Sun in this polarity might place himself at Point A as he begins to develop socially, seeking to get his own way as much as possible. But he discovers, through the law of cause and effect, that the more he tries to get his own way, the fewer friends he has. After a while this becomes painful, so he may move to Point B in the spectrum, where he begins to experiment with his opposite Libran characteristics. This wins him friends, but now he hardly ever gets his own way, which is

also painful. So he adjusts to Point C or some other point between A and B that is the most rewarding and least painful position. He is beginning to learn the art of compromise, which is
really what oppositions teach us.

As an adult he will discover that he can change his position as often as he wants in order to fit different social situations.
When he is the boss at the office, he is at Point A, but when he is
at home with his family, he switches to Point C. He also learns
frustration when something external interferes with this free and
kinetic movement between points in the spectrum. Sometimes
when the frustration becomes severe, the first signs of physical
disease begin to develop in the body, centered in the organs and
processes that are symbolically related to the area where this
major frustration is occurring.

Frustration is related to experiencing tension from being
pulled or pressured from conflicting directions. This can often be
detected from natal and transiting planets in square aspect. Thus
we see how oppositions (the need for compromise) and squares
(tension from conflict) are often important factors in reading a
horoscope for potential health problems.

Each of the natal planets in the chart, of course, occupies
its own spectrum, which works in the same way as the example
of the Sun given above. In each spectrum the individual adjusts
his position and mode of expression in response to changing conditions. Frustration of any of these planetary adjustments may
lead to manifestation in disease.

Sign Polarities

Now that we have reviewed the law of astrological
polarities, we can see how this law applies to the human body.
Before entering any of the healing professions, every student
must take two courses that are fundamental to understanding
the workings of the human body—anatomy and physiology.
Anatomy is the study of the structure, location and physical appearance of the different body tissues and organs, which are

made up of cells, the basic building blocks of life. Physiology is concerned with the processes (chemical reactions) that take place in these tissues and organs and how they interrelate to sustain life.

The six pairs of zodiac signs relate anatomically to clearly established anatomical regions of the body as well as to the tissues and organs in those regions. Each pair also corresponds to some physiological process that is essential to life. The signs and the planets in those signs form the basic alphabet of medical astrology. Following are the sign pairs and the anatomical regions that they rule. The words in italics represent the physiological functions of each pair. These keywords apply to any astrological delineation, not just medical astrology.

ARIES-LIBRA. Anatomically, Aries rules the skull, the brain, the upper teeth and everything in the head except the lower jaw. Libra rules the "belt" area at the level of the navel, which includes the kidneys, the adrenal glands and the lumbar and sacral vertebrae of the spine. Physiologically, the function of this sign pair is *regulative.* The kidneys maintain the salt and fluid balance of the body and keep toxic substances from building up to a dangerous level. The medulla oblongata contains the nerve centers that regulate heart and respiration rate, and the brain regulates all physical and mental activities.

TAURUS-SCORPIO. Anatomically, Taurus rules the lower jaw and the throat region, including the larynx (voice box), the tonsils, upper cervical vertebrae, tongue, mouth and thyroid gland. Scorpio rules the organs of reproduction, the large intestine, the rectum and, in men, the prostate gland. Physiologically, this sign pair has *consumptive, eliminative* and *procreative* functions. The solid waste products of digestion pass through the Scorpio region, and the waste products of respiration—water and carbon dioxide—pass through the mouth (Taurus region).

GEMINI-SAGITTARIUS. Gemini rules the respiratory tree (the lungs, thoracic cavity and diaphragm), the trachea (windpipe), the arms from fingers to shoulder blades, and the upper thoracic vertebrae. Sagittarius rules the hips and the upper legs down to the knees, as well as the very important sciatic nerve. The physiological functions of this sign pair are *distributive* and *locomotive*. All the body's tubes are ruled by Gemini, which moves essential body materials to the cells through the various tubes, thus ruling the body's plumbing apparatus. Sagittarius is locomotive in that it enables us to move from one place to another; for example, we could not walk without the strong muscles of the upper legs.

CANCER-CAPRICORN. This sign pair may be thought of as being both *structural* and *protective*. Cancer rules the upper abdomen and the upper portion of the liver. It also rules all of the body's containers—breasts, stomach, womb, peritoneum (the membrane encompassing the abdominal cavity), the pleural sac surrounding the thoracic cavity, the pericardium surrounding the heart, and the meninges, which are the sacs surrounding the brain and the spinal canal. Capricorn rules the knees as well as the skeleton and the skin, both of which give structure to the body. The skin and the internal membranes protect the organs within.

LEO-AQUARIUS. Anatomically, Leo rules the heart and the spinal vertebrae directly behind the heart; Aquarius rules the lower legs and ankles, as well as the oxidative process which energizes the body. Physiologically, this sign is basically *circulatory* and *energizing* in nature. The heart, by pumping blood, energizes everything within the body. This pair is responsible for the basic chemical reaction that takes place in every cell of the body: oxidation, the combination of oxygen with glucose to produce energy.

VIRGO-PISCES. Physiologically, the functions of this sign pair are *assimilative, discriminative* and *isolative*. Virgo rules the lower abdominal cavity, which includes the lower liver, pancreas, gall bladder and spleen. In this portion of the body, materials essential to nutrition are sorted out and separated from nondigestible materials. The liver also discriminates between substances that are needed and those that are toxic to the body.

Food is assimilated through the walls of the small intestine. Pisces is also discriminative, assimilative and isolative because it rules the lymphatic system, which is the body's defense against invading bacteria and viruses. The white blood cells discriminate between normal body proteins and the foreign protein of the invaders, then seek to assimilate the invaders by surrounding and isolating them. Pisces also rules the feet.

The sign polarities are important to medical astrology in a number of ways. A classic example, as reported in various astrological publications, is the observed susceptibility of persons with the Sun in Gemini to respiratory infections and diseases, especially asthma. Close behind them in this susceptibility are those with their Sun in Sagittarius, Gemini's polar opposite. Many children with severe asthma also exhibit eczema and/or inflammation of the back of the upper legs, the anatomical region of Sagittarius.

In years gone by, it was very common to remove children's tonsils, which are in the Taurus region. Today this procedure is done less routinely, for statistical studies show that males who had their tonsils removed in youth are more prone to prostate problems (the Scorpio region) in later life and that women whose tonsils were removed are more subject to problems involving the reproductive organs. Quite often, when one area of the body is diseased or operated on, the anatomical region symbolized by its opposite sign is also affected. Another example of this Taurus-Scorpio phenomenon is mumps, which affects either the glands of the throat (Taurus) or the male's testicles (Scorpio).

We could cite many other examples of this sign polarity phenomenon. Lovemaking, ruled by Taurus-Scorpio, involves both the mouth and the organs of reproduction. Both of these areas are the most susceptible to venereal disease, and Taurus and Scorpio people seem particularly susceptible to problems of this sort. Gout, which commonly affects the feet, is caused by the body's inability to eliminate the products of protein metabolism, so that uric acid builds up in the capillaries of the feet. The discriminative process (Virgo) has been altered, and the liver enzymes are involved, a classical Virgo-Pisces problem. Aries-Libra persons seem to have headache and kidney problems. Cancer-Capricorn women, especially, seem to have problems with excessive water retention (Cancer), and this fluid tends to collect in the Capricorn region. Examples of this phenomenon are legion!

Instead of memorizing the whole list of signs and related body areas, the best way to remember this symbolism is to memorize the key words in italics for each sign pair. These key words also apply to any astrological delineation, not just medical and nutritional astrology.

House Polarities

Every beginning student of astrology learns that the sixth house of the natal chart is called the health house, because of its close relationship to nutrition and potential health problems. However, as in any other astrological delineation, one must consider the *whole chart* in order to develop any meaningful conclusions. Again, the law of polarities is important in examining the house meanings.

Generally speaking, the first six houses of the chart deal with a person's individual makeup and what he or she brings to any given situation. The seventh through twelfth houses deal more with how the individual functions in the social milieu. In other words, the lower house in the polarity is what the individual brings to a particular situation, while the upper house indicates what he or she seeks from the situation.

FIRST-SEVENTH. The first house deals with the general health and physical status of the body and its physiological needs. In particular, the first house deals with health shortly after birth and the environment into which the individual is born. The location of the Ascendant represents the moment of birth, which we discuss in greater detail in Chapter Thirteen.

The first house is also associated with health conditions that relate to the head, such as problems with the teeth, eyesight and hearing, as well as baldness, acne and mental disease.

The seventh house in general relates to people we consult on a one-to-one basis; in medical astrology this house represents doctors, psychologists, chiropractors, nutritionists, astrologers and anyone else who is consulted about health problems. More specifically, the seventh represents persons consulted on any sixth-house matter. Some astrologers will certainly dispute this, because traditionally Juipiter is associated with doctors, and the ninth house, the natural house of Jupiter, is the house of experts and people consulted for their expertise, such as priests, professors and gurus. However, modern society recognizes that medical doctors are not infallible. They are no longer worshiped like tribal witch doctors nor revered, like the old country "doc," as slightly lower than God. We consult a doctor on a one-to-one basis just as we consult an astrologer, and if one does not provide an answer to our problem, we go in search of another. Thus I feel that the seventh house represents the healers we consult to restore our natural good health, which involves balance—Libra. In selecting a healer, it is wise to look for someone whose horoscope is compatible with our own seventh-house influences.

SECOND-EIGHTH. This polarity is associated most specifically with the process of reproduction and the physical act of sex. Sexual problems normally turn up in this house polarity. The second house represents what each individual brings to the sexual act, and the eighth house represents what he or she expects from a partner. In addition, the sign polarity on the cusps of these houses indicates the conditions that are most conducive to completing the sexual act. Frigidity is often related to Saturn in these houses; premature ejaculation, to Mars, fantasies, to Neptune; and so forth. Masturbation is a second-house phenomenon. Contrary to what other astrologers have reported, this house polarity has little to do with the choice of a sexual partner; instead, it represents the coming together of the partners once the partner has been selected. The selection of a sexual partner, either heterosexual or homosexual, is more a first-seventh phenomenon.

THIRD-NINTH.   This house polarity pertains to the mind, often representing conditions from which we must free or differentiate ourselves if we are to maintain good health. In fact, freedom and differentiation are good keywords for this polarity. How free are we to express ourselves and allow others to express themselves? What do we (third house) think of our health problems, and what do others (ninth house) think of them? How free are we of ties to our blood relatives and in-laws? All these questions are related to this polarity. While Saturn in one of these houses may well indicate a slow, careful and methodical thinker, it may also indicate someone who is so tied to a particular point of view ("cast in concrete") that he or she is practically incapable of changing to meet varying circumstances. A person's mental attitude has a very strong effect on the outcome of treatment for disease conditions; in fact, many healers are now coming around to the belief that most disease conditions have some mental problem as their root cause. If a patient adopts the attitude that he will die from his condition, chances are quite good that he will, for the thought is usually parent to the deed or outcome. Perhaps we ought to readjust our thinking and refer to this house polarity as the "mental health polarity," for often we must look here for the root cause of a health problem. The ultimate success of any one-to-one relationship (first-seventh), once the sexual component (second-eighth) is no longer the chief binding factor, depends on the partners' ability to communicate with each other (third-ninth). More human relationships break up because of the inability to communicate than because of any other single factor!

FOURTH-TENTH.   This house polarity concerns a person's feeling of security within himself (fourth house) and the security or lack of it provided by others. Part of this security comes from the individual's foundation and ancestry and part from his ultimate success and acceptance as an individual (tenth house).

The fourth house, for example, deals with the surname. A person whose surname begins with a letter near the beginning of the alphabet is conditioned by society to be first; a person whose name begins with a letter near the end is conditioned to be last and is therefore often more patient in awaiting the outcome of events.

This polarity also deals with the influence of the mother and father upon this individual's development and his ability to form partnerships and develop his own identity. As doctors learn more about the conditions leading to heart attack, arthritis, cancer and other diseases, they are beginning to recognize that these diseases are related to the individual's ability to express emotions and feelings, and to the way the individual sees himself in the society to which he belongs. From this house polarity we gain insight into how the individual functions in society and whether he views himself as a success or failure. Thus a good keyword for this polarity is recognition.

FIFTH-ELEVENTH. The result of sexual union (second-eighth) and the value the individual places upon one-to-one relationships (first-seventh) is manifest in this house polarity, which concerns offspring and the ability to love another and accept love in return. The fifth house is the ceremony of courtship and all that we associate with nonsexual romance. It represents our creative abilities and instincts. The eleventh house represents nonsexual relationships with others, friendships and social activities. It also represents the achievement of hopes and wishes stemming from our creative potential.

Saturn in this polarity often creates some blockage in the free flow of energy until we learn that responsibility must accompany achievement. Jupiter here often leads us to expect too much from our efforts; Mars creates impatience in achievement; and Neptune leads us to look for the ideal, resulting in disappointment when the results are less than expected. This polarity is greatly concerned with our basic need to belong.

SIXTH-TWELFTH. Because the sixth house is the midpoint of the horoscope, this is where the individual contacts the external world, which may best be seen from the nutritional viewpoint. The sixth house is where the individual puts food into the mouth, the point at which something external to the self is taken in and eventually integrated ito the physical body. In general astrology textbooks, the twelfth house is usually spoken of as man's attempt to find his place (integrate himself) in the universe and answer the three basic questions of philosophy: Why am I here? Where did I come from? Where am I going? Thus, the real keyword for this house polarity is integration in contrast to diferentiation, the keyword for the third-ninth polarity.

The individual's ability to find his place in society and in the universal scheme of things can be read in the sixth-twelfth house polarity. But man has conflicting desires; not only does he want to find his place in society, he also craves recognition as a unique individual, as a being who is in some way different from the herd. This conflict is illustrated by the fact that the third-ninth and sixth-twelfth house polarities are in square aspect to each other within the horoscope wheel.

Secondary keywords for the sixth-twelfth house polarity are: work, health and service. How well does the individual integrate himself in situations in which he must work cooperatively with others, as in a job? How well does the individual integrate foreign substances (food) into himself? Service can be thought of as giving some portion of the self to others (sixth house) and accepting the service of others (twelfth house) in return. All of the many keywords that we commonly associate with the twelfth house—hospitals, jails, libraries, research (the prior discoveries of others), welfare—represent society serving us. Even pain and suffering, also associated with the twelfth house, really serve us by building character (first house).

I believe that a more intensive understanding of house phenomena will reveal that good health stems from the ability to *integrate* ourselves successfully into society and the universe and at the same time to *differentiate* ourselves from everyone and everything else in the universe. The health of the body depends upon how well the various organs perform their different functions and at the same time work as units of the whole. The success of a society depends basically upon these same abilities. Individuals and societies that perform both functions well survive; those that cannot, pass into obscurity.

Through education, travel and communication, we attempt to differentiate ourselves from other members of society (third-ninth). Through work and service we attempt to integrate ourselves into society (sixth-twelfth). When we are able to accomplish these tasks with minimum interference and frustration, our health is good; interference and frustration in these efforts can result in the physical manifestation of health problems.

How well the physical body is able to function depends upon how well we serve it and upon how well the mind is able to function. We think of the mind and the body as distinct and separate entities, and yet it is surely obvious, even to the untrained observer, that neither body nor mind can function without the other; they are inextricably interdependent. Astrology confirms this interdependence.

The Symbolism of the Planets

As we know from basic astrology, each of the ten planets symbolizes some energy that must be expressed in our life if we are to realize our truest and highest potential. Blocking or frustrating the expression of such energy usually causes pain in one form or another and, as we pointed out earlier, disease. In addition to the matters that are usually assigned to the different planets, each one rules a particular body system and one or more of the vital endocrine glands.

THE SUN. The Sun principally symbolizes the body's basic vitality or life force. Its house position indicates in part the individual's vitality and resistance to disease. Sextiles and trines to the Sun tend to increase this resistance; squares, oppositions and inconjuncts detract from it. When the Sun is in an angular house, especially the first house, vitality is greatest; when it is in a cadent house, vitality is lowered, especially in the sixth or the twelfth house. In a succedent house, the Sun indicates a neutral situation, neither particularly strong nor particularly weak. The Sun is also symbolic of the whole circulatory system, especially the heart. The Sun's sign location indicates the regions of the body that are the most subject to malfunction and disease. Of course, since we can never neglect the law of polarities, we must also consider the region of the body ruled by the sign opposite the Sun's sign.

THE MOON. The Moon is symbolic of the emotions and their role in maintaining bodily health. It symbolizes all reflexes (acts that don't require conscious thought) and the habit patterns that we develop. Planets in conjunction with the Moon in the natal chart often indicate habit patterns that are difficult to break. The Moon, along with Cancer, the sign that it rules, is associated with all allergic conditions. It also represents the fluid portion of the body, including plasma, which is the fluid portion of the blood; all bodily secretions; the fluid waste products, sweat and urine; and the water that is part of the body.

MERCURY. Mercury was called the "messenger of the gods," and as you might expect, this planet rules the transmission of messages from one part of the body to another. Messages are transmitted electrically via the nervous system and chemically via hormones in the bloodstream. Thus Mercury rules the central nervous system and the hormonal system. It is also symbolic of logic and conscious reasoning. Mercury also rules the thyroid gland and, along with Gemini, the respiratory system.

VENUS. As the goddess of love, Venus rules physical sensations and the sensory organs. These organs connect the physical functions of the body with the mental functions, just as Taurus, ruled by Venus, connects Aries, the physical body, with Gemini, the mind. This process ends, of course, in Cancer, ruled by the Moon (the emotional reaction to external stimuli). Venus also rules the female genitalia and the venous portion of the circulatory system, the deoxygenated blood returning to the heart. Hair as an extension of the sensory system is ruled by Venus; as a protective device, it is ruled by Saturn.

MARS. The god of war and battle, Mars implies physical action and movement, and its principal rulership is the muscular system. Since the heart is also a muscle, Mars is a secondary ruler of the heart along with the Sun and Leo. Mars rules the red blood cells, which carry oxygen to the cells, providing them with energy, and it rules the adrenal glands, located above the kidneys. The hormones secreted by the adrenal glands mobilize the body's defenses when the individual is externally threatened. Mars, representing the male principle, rules the male genitalia. Venus represents the female principle.

JUPITER. Jupiter, the ruler of the gods, has as its principal function the growth and expansion of the body. It rules the arterial portion of the circulatory system; the pancreas, which governs fat production and assimilation of carbohydrates; and the liver, which is the largest organ after the skin and which performs hundreds of different chemical processes that sustain life and growth.

SATURN. This planet and the sign that it rules, Capricorn, in general are concerned with form, structure and establishing limits. Therefore, in medical astrology Saturn is the ruler of the skeletal system, which gives the body support and form, like the girders of a building. Saturn also rules the skin, which in addition to giving form and structure also establishes the boundary between the body and its environment and protects the internal structures from water loss and invasion by foreign substances. Saturn rules the parathyroid glands in the neck, which regulate the metabolism of minerals necessary to bone formation. Whereas Jupiter represents the growth process, Saturn represents the process of aging.

URANUS. Because of their relatively recent discovery, the roles of the three outer planets, Uranus, Neptune and Pluto, are not as clearly established as those of the planets known to the ancients. However, their symbolism in medical astrology has been clearly defined through observation.

Uranus rules the involuntary or autonomic nervous system, which controls the involuntary functions of the body such as digestion, respiration and heartbeat. Its principal control is over the smooth muscles (note the relationship to Mars, which rules the muscles, and to Mercury, which rules the nervous system). In this capacity Uranus has been connected with ESP and other extrasensory abilities, especially intuition, which some feel is related to the autonomic nervous system. Uranus is often considered to signify sudden, unexpected injuries to the body.

NEPTUNE. Neptune rules the spinal canal, and along with the Moon, the spinal fluid. It is the undisputed ruler of the pineal body, which is located near the top of the skull just beneath the fontanel (the opening in the skull that ossifies and closes shortly after birth). Neptune has also been associated with various ESP processes.

Perhaps most important, Neptune, which is classically called the "planet of deception," rules poisons and drugs. Any substance introduced into the body's chemical system that has no normal role in nutrition is said to be ruled by Neptune. These substances "deceive" the body in that the body perceives them as natural substances and reacts in some abnormal way. The caffeine in coffee, which resembles adrenalin, and aspirin are examples of Neptunian compounds. Aspirin "deceives" the body by turning off the sensation of pain without eliminating the source of the pain, which is one of nature's danger signals. Alcohol and anesthetics are ruled by Neptune, as are all substances that we classify as poisons, including hallucinogenic drugs.

PLUTO. Pluto's body rulerships have not yet been completely settled, because the planet was not discovered until 1930. Its rulership of the excretory system is undisputed, and it is also thought by many to rule the pituitary gland, the master gland that controls growth, hormonal secretion, and development of secondary sex characteristics at puberty. Because Pluto rules the growth hormones, some astrologers have assigned midgets, giants and other unusual growth anomalies to Pluto.

Pluto rules abnormal cell growth—tumors, birthmarks, warts, moles and the like. It is said to rule all replicative processes and thus also rules the enzymes, which catalyze chemical reactions within the cell, and the hereditary component, DNA in particular, of the cell's nucleus. Pluto is also thought to rule all foreign biological substances that enter the body, such as bacteria, fungi, viruses, protozoa and parasitic organisms. This planet is perhaps best thought of as being "the alpha and the omega" of life, representing both conception, when sperm fuses with ovum, and the death of the physical body. It is certainly implicated in all hereditary processes.

The principle of polarity applies to the planets as well as to the houses and signs. Poisons (Neptune) destroy enzymes (Pluto). One way to lose weight (excessive fat, ruled by Jupiter) is to go on a high-protein (Saturn) diet. Muscular activity, ruled by Mars, burns up sugar (Venus).

The Aspects and Health

No discussion of traditional astrological concepts would be complete without some mention of the various aspects. All of the traditionally used aspects play some role in our interpretation of health; however, the opposition, square, quincunx (or inconjunct), conjunction and semisquare are the key aspects in isolating potential health problems in the natal chart. While the source of a problem may well be some mental or psychological factor, the body often translates this frustration or tension into the physical manifestation of disease.

OPPOSITION. The opposition has traditionally been interpreted as symbolizing the need for *compromise* in the house and sign polarity in which the opposition is located. Oppositional problems are resolved through compromise between the individual and another individual or other external factors. Such problems are *interpersonal* in nature. If the individual does not reach a successful compromise, the problem may manifest in the physical symptoms of disease. A third-ninth house opposition, for example, indicates that the individual should listen to what others have to say (ninth house) and also express himself through communication (third house). It takes two to make a conversation. A person who will not listen to others, or who is afraid to communicate his feelings and thoughts to others, may express this frustration physically as a disease. To be loved by others (eleventh house) requires that one love in return (fifth house). An opposition in this polarity may symbolize some problem in the free exchange of love, and when a successful compromise is not attained, again we may find a physical manifestation in disease.

SQUARE. The square symbolizes *tension* and conflicting desires in the individual. It is more personal in nature than the opposition. A third-sixth house square, for example, represents some basic tension between the individual's need to differentiate and the need to integrate, which often results in physical manifestations. The tension is relieved by expressing both needs in situations where one will not conflict with the other, rather than by continually suppressing one of the forces. With a third-sixth house square, this could mean learning to serve others without losing one's personal identity in a blind master-slave relationship. You must know who you are and why you serve.

QUINCUNX OR INCONJUNCT. This is the 150° aspect, which is often symbolic of health problems and is usually quite prominent in death charts. While we know that the quincunx is decidedly a health aspect, we still have much to learn about its underlying psychological roots in the personality. It seems to symbolize one's attempt to put together unrelated facets of life in a fashion that makes sense to the individual. Often it is symbolic of "lots of smoke but little fire"—tremendous effort without discernible success. The frustration resulting from such effort can manifest in physical symptoms of disease. It is not uncommon for health problems involving the quincunx to be conquered suddenly, or a remission to take place when one of the slower-moving planets by transit conjuncts one of the planets forming the quincunx. Psychologically, the quincunx has been interpreted as the desire to have that which we cannot have, or frustration of one's efforts to reach a desired goal, although it may be attained quite late in life and only after many defeats.

CONJUNCTION. In traditional astrology, the conjunction symbolizes the fusion or joining together of two planetary forces. Depending upon the planets and the forces they symbolize, as well as the way the individual handles the problem, the conjunction may be beneficial or may present a potential problem. A good example is the conjunction of the Sun with Neptune. On the one hand, this conjunction can indicate an individual with great imagination, someone who can see beyond the realm of the average person, or it can symbolize the hypochondriac who reads about some disease in *Reader's Digest* and is certain that he has that disease. Conjunctions of a planet and the Moon must be carefully considered. The Moon represents our habit patterns, and a planet in conjunction with the Moon often symbolizes some habit pattern that cannot easily be broken. For example, the Moon conjunct Neptune often indicates problems with drugs, alcohol, or smoking, because once the habit is formed it is not easily broken. The individual doesn't realize how injurious the habit is until it is too late. A smoker may know full well that smoking can lead to lung cancer, but he fantasizes that "it will never happen to me!"

SEMISQUARE. Most astrologers do not classify the semisquare (45°) among the major aspects; nevertheless, in interpreting health problems it cannot be overlooked, for it is often an indicator of friction. In and of itself, the semisquare does not usually indicate major problems, but in combination with other factors in the chart, it sometimes indicates contributing causes of some health condition. In my experience, a semisquare between a transiting and a natal planet is of particular importance as a triggering influence that brings on an unhealthy condition. In any case, the semisquare aspect should not be ignored.

Astrological Signatures of Disease

Some disease conditions—hemophilia, for example—are congenital or natal in origin, having their onset at the time of conception; some, such as defects caused by thalidomide, develop while the fetus is in the uterine environment. The pattern, or astrological "signature," of a congenital disease or condition is usually found wholly in the natal chart. A disease that develops later in life is usually shown by a picture or signature formed by the natal planets, which show a predisposition to the condition, with transiting and sometimes progressed planets completing the picture at the date of onset.

At this point I want to examine an idea that is being pursued by many astrologers, which is that if one compares the accurate horoscopes of a number of persons who have a particular disease, one ought to find a consistent planetary picture in each one. It is an interesting assumption, which has led me up many blind alleys and resulted in countless hours of fruitless study. On the basis of my own long observation, I can only conclude that in the light of our present knowledge there is no single, consistent planetary picture for any disease condition. There are no "cookbook" signatures for any health problems, despite claims made to the contrary in such books as *Medical Astrology* by Omar Garrison. Anyone willing to test out the signatures Garrison provides can quickly verify my findings, as a number of my associates have already done.

However, there does seem to be some evidence that certain general health conditions are related to the sign polarity in which the Sun is located. For example, those with the Sun in Gemini-Sagittarius seem to have a particular sensitivity to respiratory problems, especially asthma. To a lesser extent, this also holds true for certain Ascendants. A large number of my clients with Capricorn rising have mentioned having hearing problems at some time in their lives. These are not "categorical statements," and they are not substantiated by any hard evidence; however, it seems to me that pursuing such studies in an organized scientific manner would be of much more potential benefit than the search for specific signatures of disease.

There is considerable controversy as to whether the positions of the major fixed stars have any real meaning in the general delineation of the horoscope, or whether they can safely be overlooked. Again, according to my own observation, they cannot and should not be overlooked, though again this is a fertile area for serious statistical work. One fixed star, Praesepe at about 7°Leo, has particularly impressed me in this regard. According to Cornell's *Encyclopedia of Medical Astrology*, this fixed star, or at least this particular degree, is often associated with blindness, either from birth, when a natal planet is located at 7° (±1°) Leo, or later, when this degree is set off by transit. More than this single factor is involved, of course, and many persons with a natal or transiting planet at 7° Leo have perfectly good eyesight; nevertheless, I have twenty-three charts in my collection for blindness, and every single one has a conjunction of some sort with Praesepe at 7° Leo! To any scientifically trained person, this evidence, although not impressive in quantity at this point, would indicate a fruitful area of further investigation. I am certainly not willing to write off the fixed stars at this point, and I would not like my colleagues to do so either.

A basic principle of astrological delineation is that any given condition or situation appears symbolically in several different ways in the natal chart. This principle certainly applies in any serious study of the chart for health purposes. There are usually a number of different combinations that lead to certain inescapable conclusions. The particular combinations are hard to catalog, and the only one who has come close to doing so is Dr. Cornell in his *Encyclopedia of Medical Astrology*. I am quite aware that astrology's companion science, cosmobiology, has also made some important attempts at cataloging certain health conditions as they relate to planetary midpoints and particular degrees of the zodiac. However, in my opinion, the cosmobiological findings need considerably more research before any of their conclusions can be considered as "signatures" for health problems.

3

ASTRO-NUTRITIONAL THEORY

In this chapter we discuss how to apply the symbolism of astrology to nutrition. In subsequent chapters we take up the various steps in nutrition in more detail. You may think that nutrition begins when you place food in your mouth and start to chew it. However, both astrology and nutrition make it very clear that the process of nutrition starts long before this. It starts on the farm or ranch with the raising of crops or animals and continues through the intermediate processing steps and the final cooking of the food. What the animals are fed, what fertilizers are used in growing the crops, whether pesticides are used, what preservatives and other artificial materials are added by the food processor—all these factors are important in understanding the whole process of nutrition.

Nutrition and the Houses

Let's look at the first steps in nutrition in terms of astrology. Basic astrological theory teaches us that each sign and each house prepares the way for the next sign and the next house—the next step.

The first six houses of the horoscope represent the personal side of your nature (yourself in relationship to you); the last six, the interpersonal side of our nature (yourself in relationship to others). The first quadrant, houses one, two and three, represents what you are born with: the first house, the physical body; the second, the senses, which connect the physical body with the mind; and the third, the intellect.

The second house represents what you value. It is the natural house of Taurus, and Taurus is ruled by Venus, which represents the sensory organs. It is precisely these organs that we use to determine what foods we like and dislike. Taste is certainly one of these senses, but smell, the visual appearance and the texture of the food we eat are also important in our reactions to food. And who does not enjoy hearing bacon frying or being complimented on a meal well prepared and served? All five senses are involved in eating, and all five senses are ruled by Venus—the pleasure principle. Taurus has always been symbolic of the gourmet.!

The second quadrant, houses four, five and six, represents the fulfillment of your personal needs from resources outside of yourself. The fourth house, whose natural sign ruler is Cancer, represents the nurturing of life, motherhood, security and family tradition. It also governs the soil, the dairy industry, milk and food processing. The individual, as represented by the first three houses, must be given a chance to grow and mature, and the signs Cancer through Virgo represent the summer months when growth flourishes.

From the security provided by the mother—the fourth house—the child comes to feel loved—the fifth house—and is able to offer himself in love to others. Leo, ruler of the heart, is the natural ruler of the fifth house. This house also represents our creativity within the food preparation process. Leo is a fire sign, and heating or cooking is a very important part of food preparation; this is where the cook (fourth house) expresses his or her creativity. The sign on the cusp of the fifth house in your horoscope symbolizes the style with which you prepare the food you eat. (The United States, born on July Fourth, is a Cancer-Sun nation, and it is basic to the American tradition that love is expressed by serving a good meal.)

The sixth house, of course, represents what happens to

the food when you put it in your mouth as well as your eating habits and the conditions surrounding mealtimes. We have already pointed out that Virgo and its natural house represent your diet. Virgo, the ruler of nutrition, is symbolized by the grain of wheat. Consider its opposite sign, Pisces, symbolized by the fishes. It is interesting that in the symbolism of the Bible, Christ fed the multitudes with the loaves—Virgo—and fishes—Pisces.

Crossing the horizon, we move into the upper hemisphere and the third quadrant, houses seven, eight and nine. The seventh house represents how well your body is able to regulate and balance (Libra) your diet against your individual daily requirements.

The eighth house represents how you finally eliminate the materials that the body cannot use (Scorpio). The ninth house represents the results of the whole nutritional process in growth and maturation (Sagittarius and Jupiter). Each sign and house leads to the next step in the process.

The fourth and final quadrant includes the tenth, eleventh and twelfth houses. The tenth house is where the individual, having satisfied his needs and grown to maturity, is able to productively utilize his or her time. Here the mature adult works and earns a reputation based upon the "fruits of his labor." Astrologers often refer to the second, sixth and tenth houses as the material or business houses, because they are said to represent your business acumen. We may also call them the

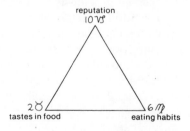

Figure 1. The Nutritional Triangle.

nutritional houses, because they are symbolic of your nutritional tastes and habits; taking responsibility for these aspects of nutrition results in your physical well-being.

The eleventh and twelfth houses, being opposite the fifth and sixth, indicate your acknowledgment of membership rights and obligations within society and, finally, within the cosmos. Through the sacrifices you make, as shown by the twelfth house, you become a source of life and sustainment for all future generations.

Signs on the Sixth House Cusp

Let's look at some of the factors of the nutritional triangle as they pertain to your own chart. Normally the second, sixth and tenth house signs are all in the same element; you will have to make allowances for charts in which intercepted signs disturb this natural relationship.

ARIES. Typically you're a "hit and run" eater, eating whenever you are hungry rather than at scheduled times each day. You usually prefer your food hot and spicy, and you tend to gobble your food without chewing it adequately. You're less likely than others to plan a balanced diet. You're a protein eater, and you need more meat in your diet and more foods that are high in iron than the average individual. With Aries here, you have a Scorpio Ascendant and are normally not one to remark that you enjoyed your meal; in truth you don't much care whether the meal is served graciously or tastefully. Your tendency is just to dig in, and you are usually the first to leave the table once you are full. You hate to cook, and when you do, you tend to overcook your food. You are likely to be a regular customer at McDonald's and other fast-food establishments, for you hate to stand in line and wait for a meal. Your tastes in food are basically Sagittarian, and you especially like foods that are boiled.

With Leo on your tenth house cusp, you will find that a creatively prepared, appetizing dinner is enjoyable and has a calming effect. Warm, lightly seasoned foods with little salt will promote better digestion and nutrition.

TAURUS. No question about it—you're the gourmet! You eat slowly and like to savor what you eat. Typically you're not picky about foods you eat, as long as they are well prepared. However, you have a tendency to overeat, and your keen taste for desserts may incline you to become rather plump as you get older. You have Sagittarius rising, and thus Jupiter is your chart ruler. Jupiter inclines to excesses, and the result of dietary excess is fat—also ruled by Jupiter! Sagittarius, however, inclines you to be rather tall, with a large frame, so excess fat is not as obvious. You have the satisfaction of knowing that with Sagittarius rising, if you watch your diet, you may live longer than other people. Capricorn rules your taste, which probably includes a fondness for mushrooms, sour or acid foods like sauerkraut and pickles, cold foods like ices and ice cream, and gourmet foods from other countries.

With Virgo on the tenth house cusp, the point of nutritional balance, you should pay close attention to what you eat. Identify and avoid any foods that make you feel uncomfortable after eating. Eating too much food (Taurus) or concentrating too much on how the meal is served (Capricorn) will disturb your metabolic balance.

GEMINI. You're inclined to eat when you feel like it rather than at scheduled times; in other words, you're a snacker. Both men and women with Gemini here like to cook and prepare meals for others. And while they're cooking they nibble, so by the time the meal is ready, they're generally full. Mealtime for you is a time for good conversation, discussing the day's activities around the table. With Capricorn rising, good form is important, and you notice good manners and insist upon them in your children. Your tastes in food are basically Aquarian, and since Aquarius rules salt, you like your foods well salted, which is not conducive to good nutrition. Your tastes in food change often, and thus you require great variety, but you are willing to try almost any food at least once.

A balanced diet is your key to good nutrition, with Libra on the tenth house cusp. You should plan each meal to include foods from each of the four nutritional groups.

CANCER. Like Taurus, you love good food and large family gatherings at mealtimes. Your tastes in food tend toward the traditional. Probably you have a large collection of recipes, some of which have been handed down through the family for generations, and you take pride in your cooking, especially of desserts. Cancers are cake and pie bakers—and eaters. Dairy products are probably an important part of your meals. You like to see others leave the table "stuffed," and if children are around, you probably keep a jar full of cookies for them. If you have Capricorn rising, you also have many of the characteristics mentioned in the description of Gemini on the sixth house cusp, with rather fixed tastes in food. If you "brown bag" it at work, you're inclined to stick to the same foods day after day with little variety. But if Aquarius or, for some, Capricorn, is rising, Pisces occupies your second house, which means you enjoy seafoods, since Pisces symbolizes fish and the sea. Pisces is changeable, so you need plenty of variety in your diet; what tastes good today can lose its appeal tomorrow. Alcoholic beverages, fried foods and oily salads also appeal to you, but excesses of all three should be avoided for good nutrition and health.

With Scorpio on your tenth house, the key to good nutrition is proper elimination. Be sure to include foods that add bulk, such as salads and bran. Ilnesses may be caused by a buildup of toxic waste products, so you should promote elimination. Periodic fasting and/or occasional use of a mild laxative may enhance your feeling of well-being.

LEO. Those with Leo here, the sun-worshipers, like their food well cooked and hot, served in warm surroundings with lots of pomp and ceremony. You enjoy eating out at the most lavish places your pocketbook will permit. You are attracted to supper clubs and cabarets that provide entertainment with the meal. When you entertain, there is always plenty of food for the guests. You put on good parties, which people generally enjoy.

With Pisces rising, you usually provide lots of liquor too, if you can afford it. "Lavish" is the best word to describe your eating habits. When you shop, you're inclined to pick the most colorful, fresh, sun-ripened foods and the best cuts of meat you can afford. With Cancer on the fifth house, you may well have the reputation of being a good cook. Garlic, lamb, mustard and rhubarb should appeal to your taste, since they are all ruled by Aries (on your second house of taste).

With Sagittarius on your tenth house cusp, you should get plenty of exercise for good health. After a heavy meal, a brisk walk will aid digestion and make you feel good. If you do not exercise enough, you will tend to feel full and sluggish after eating, which may lead to buildup of toxic wastes.

VIRGO.   The pickiness of Virgo is most noticeable on the cusp of the sixth, its natural house. Many nutritionists have Virgo here, and if you're typical, you are the family nutritionist. You are concerned that everyone around you eat a balanced diet, well supplemented by vitamins and other dietary needs. Many with Virgo here are vegetarians or follow some other rather strict dietary regimen. You like to serve your meals on time or on a fixed schedule. People with this placement seem to be continually on a diet and watch their calorie intake carefully. Since Aries rises, your patience with others' eating habits is rather short. Beans, cereals and pork products should especially suit your taste, with Taurus on your second house. With Leo on the cusp of your fifth house, you like your food colorfully prepared and steaming hot.

Capricorn on your tenth house cusp is a reminder of an often-neglected factor in good nutrition--proper posture. At meals, be sure to sit in a chair that makes you sit up straight, and afterward, be sure to sit or stand with a straight back. By paying more attention to your posture at all times, you can often avoid many minor digestive problems.

LIBRA.   With Libra here, mealtimes are the occasion for good conversation and sociability. When you entertain, food is not so important, although you usually have plenty of candy

47

around. You are the cocktail-party variety of entertainer. With Virgo on the fifth house cusp, though, you are a stickler for properly prepared meals. If Taurus rises, you can be a slave to habit in that you are not very willing to try new foods. Potatoes, ruled by Venus, may well be a mainstay of your diet. Archie Bunker at the dinner table is the symbol of this placement. Typically, you have a sweet tooth, and gifts of candy are always welcome. This combination tends to make you overweight, so count your calories carefully. With Gemini on your second house cusp, you like nuts, and in meats, the rib and shoulder cuts. This combination best symbolizes America's eating habits.

Aquarius, the water bearer, on your tenth house cusp suggests the need to include more liquids in your diet. Liquids aid in good digestion by washing excess salts out of your system, and constipation may be a problem unless you increase your intake of liquids.

SCORPIO. This is the sign of the "loner," and Pluto, its ruler, symbolizes dark and out-of-the-way places. Dark, intimate and unusual eating places off the beaten path should appeal to you. You don't mind eating alone or with just one other person by candlelight in romantic surroundings. Something to drink with meals, alcoholic or otherwise, is a must. With Cancer on your second house, you're probably a milk drinker. You love dairy products of all sorts as well as oysters (often raw), macaroni, noodles, eggs and mushrooms. Many people with Virgo on the fourth-house cusp enjoy growing their own vegetables in a backyard garden. A peculiarity of this combination is that you tend to eat when you feel like it, and when you get hungry, nothing can keep you from eating. You are very compulsive about eating times and food selection; when you are hungry you don't like to be kept waiting.

With Pisces on your tenth house cusp, you tend to assume that your diet is providing what you need, because you are more interested in other areas of life. With Gemini rising, you should focus your attention more on your diet and take responsibility for your own nutrition. It can be a fascinating study, and with your intellectual curiosity, it is certainly worthy of your attention.

SAGITTARIUS. With Jupiter ruling the sixth house, this combination is symbolized by the horn of plenty. Your table groans under the weight of the food. Your family will never go hungry as long as you have a nickel in your pocket, and in-laws may be frequent guests at your table. Foods from abroad whet your appetite. There is also a tendency to overeat, and few people with this combination can be called skinny. When you prepare meals, you like everyone else to stay out of the kitchen. With Leo on the cusp of your second house, your tastes include almonds, cinnamon, corn, gin, citrus fruits, olives, rice and foods grown on vines, such as grapes and squash.

Aries on your tenth house cusp emphasizes the need to pay more attention to your physical body. Are you proud of your body? With Cancer rising, you are sensitive about what others think of you, and a bad self-image can drive you back into your shell. You take great pride in your possessions, but remember, your greatest possession is your body. By taking pride in it and paying attention to good bodily nutrition, you can gain greater self-confidence and security.

CAPRICORN. You tend to be careful about what you eat, and you are able to leave the table when you are full. You are concerned with form, good manners and how the meal is served; Leo rising complements this. When you eat out, you choose a place where you will be noticed socially, and you are usually not a bit hesitant about sending food back to the kitchen. You like to transact business at the dinner table and you rarely drink too much, if at all. Virgo on the second house makes your tastes even more fussy. Honey, poultry and grain foods satisfy your Virgo tastes well. While you may not be a gourmet, you are likely to be a connoisseur of food and drink, an excellent coffee and wine taster.

Taurus on the cusp of your tenth house means that your taste is a good indicator of what is best for you to eat. If something doesn't taste good, you probably shouldn't eat it.

Listen to what your taste buds tell you about what is best for you nutritionally.

AQUARIUS.   Quite a number of people with Aquarius, the sign of service, in the house of service, work in the food industry, frequently as waiters and waitresses. You are particularly careful about how you prepare food for yourself and others, and you like to experiment with new, and sometimes rather zany, dishes. You are budget conscious and know how to get the best value for your food dollar. With Libra on the second house cusp, sweets can sometimes be a problem. You enjoy strawberries and like to have music with your meals.

The duality of Gemini, which is on the cusp of your tenth house, controls your nutrition. At one moment, you are very careful about the kinds of food you eat, but at the next, you overindulge in junk foods that have no food value. Overindulgence in sweets and carbohydrates is likely to be your greatest problem. However, Virgo rising gives you the ability to discriminate and to choose your diet wisely.

PISCES.   Individuals with Pisces here eat when they feel like it, when the mood strikes them. You like alcohol, but you are often diet conscious, because with Libra rising, you want to maintain an attractive physical appearance. With Scorpio on the second house cusp, your tastes in food are fixed, with definite likes and dislikes. You eat plenty of protein. You are not a candy eater and rarely eat desserts, but you do love licorice. You fit in easily with any social group at mealtime and enjoy good conversation while eating, but when you are really hungry, you tend to bolt your food without chewing it properly. Normally you enjoy cooking for and entertaining others at meals. You tend to oversalt your foods. You also enjoy growing your own vegetables in a backyard garden. Guests who eat with you had better compliment the chef, or they are not likely to get another invitation; those with Libra rising thrive on flattery!

Cancer on your tenth house cusp indicates a need to drink plenty of liquids with your meals. With Libra rising, balance is essential in your diet, and you should balance solid foods with enough liquids to aid digestion. Food allergies and gas are indicators of an unbalanced diet. Also you tend to eat when you are feeling insecure or to drink when you are tense, but it is not good to try to escape your problems by eating. Your emotions at mealtimes affect your digestion, so try to create a pleasant atmosphere when you eat.

Food Allergies

Every health-oriented astrologer knows that allergies are primarily symbolized by the Moon and by Cancer. Those with the Moon in the sixth house or Cancer on its cusp frequently report allergic reactions to certain types of foods. They are likely to be allergic to dairy products, especially milk, although they may like these foods anyway.

Watch also for any planets in the horoscope that are in square aspect to the Moon, for the foods symbolized by the aspecting planet may cause food allergies. Jupiter or Venus square the Moon in the sixth house, for example, sometimes indicates an allergic reaction to strawberries.

I have observed that many persons with Gemini on the cusp of the sixth house also suffer from food allergy, because Cancer occupies the latter degrees of this house. Asthma, in particular, can be brought on by certain foods.

Sun Sign Variations

In general, all humans have the same general nutritional requirements; however, because of heredity we require differing proportions of the various essential foods, because we digest some substances easily and others with some difficulty. Your natal Sun sign indicates foods that are metabolized easily; the sign opposite the Sun sign indicates foods that are not metabolized easily.

However, if a person increases the proportion of the foods symbolized by the sign opposite the Sun sign, there is little benefit unless the substances related to the Sun sign are also present to enhance their metabolism.

For example, people with the Sun in Cancer require increased calcium in the diet, since calcium is ruled by Saturn, which also rules Capricorn, Cancer's opposite sign. To take calcium tablets alone would have little effect; the calcium should be obtained through milk, dairy products and other Cancer-ruled substances. Mother Nature in her wisdom provides for this, because persons with a Cancer Sun are usually fond of dairy products! This principle is further demonstrated in Chapters Nine and Ten, which discuss vitamins, minerals, and the physiological cell salts.

Be careful not to confuse these nutritional requirements with the food preferences discussed earlier.The Sun and its opposite sign show special nutritional *requirements,* which have little to do with your particular food preferences and tastes as shown by the sign on the second house cusp. Often we want foods that are not particularly good for us nor easily digestible, especially when the signs on the cusps of the second and tenth houses are in different elements because of interception.

Astrology and Metabolism

The student should keep in mind certain basic principles in studying astro-nutrition. First of all, the word metabolism represents the sum of all the biochemical processes that take place within the body. These processes can be divided into two general categories of chemical reaction: processes that break down complex compounds into simpler ones and those that make simpler compounds into more complex ones. The biologist calls these processes catabolism and anabolism, respectively; the chemist calls them analysis and synthesis. But whatever you call these two processes, Venus/Jupiter is symbolically related to the anabolic processes, and Mars/Saturn to the catabolic processes. In the simplest terms, Venus represents the process of growing, and Jupiter represents the result—growth. Mars represents the degenerative processes, and Saturn their result—old age and eventual death.

Another way of looking at metabolism is in terms of energy. Some reactions use energy; other reactions release energy. The majority of chemical reactions in the body require energy in order to occur. These, called endothermic reactions, are under the general rulership of the Moon. Exothermic reactions, those that release energy, are ruled by the Sun. Most exothermic reactions involve oxidation of some compound; when the compound combines with oxygen, heat is released. The basic process of respiration is exothermic, with the simple sugar glucose as the fuel and with the blood supplying oxygen. The heat that is released provides each cell with the necessary energy for all of its endothermic reactions.

In broad terms, respiration is ruled by the Sun, but it is also a Saturn-ruled process (analysis), because the relatively complex glucose molecule is broken down into the simpler molecules of carbon dioxide and water. The reverse endothermic process in plants is called photosynthesis, in which the plant combines the Sun's energy with water and carbon dioxide to form starch in its leaves. Photosynthesis is ruled by the Moon and by Jupiter (synthesis).

Digestion is also a two-part process. In the first part, foods are broken down from complex to simpler compounds. What takes place along the digestive tract is analytic and Saturn-ruled. After these simple compounds are absorbed in the small intestine, their rearrangement into more complex compounds that the body needs is synthetic and thus Jupiter-ruled.

Therefore, in assessing a natal horoscope for nutritional or metabolic purposes it is most important to note the aspect relationships among the Sun, Moon, Venus, Mars, Jupiter and Saturn. Sometimes the so-called afflicted aspects—specifically, planets in square, opposition, semisquare or quincunx (inconjunct)—indicate problems with the body chemistry. A conjunction between planets in group one (Sun, Venus, Jupiter) and group two (Moon, Mars, Saturn) is also an aspect of affliction.

A conjunction within one of these groups is not generally considered an affliction, at least from the nutritional point of view.

In nutritional astrology, Mercury and Uranus generally symbolize mental aspects of the physical problem. Neptune and Pluto are usually associated with compounds that in one way or another are toxic to the body or at least have no part in the body's natural chemistry. Neptune represents drugs that "deceive" the body in some way to accomplish some medical purpose. Aspirin, for example, is Neptune-ruled, since it makes the body turn off the pain mechanism and tricks the senses into believing that the pain is gone. Neptune-type poisons are those that we do not usually identify as poisons; Pluto-type poisons are as a rule more obvious. Pluto is also the general ruler of enzymes, but the purpose of enzymes is to cause certain reactions to occur; they are not themselves products of the reaction.

In Saturn-type reactions (analysis), solid or gaseous waste products are formed that are of no further value to the body and must be eliminated. The solid waste products are ruled by Pluto, and the gaseous ones by Neptune. These waste products can be toxic to the body if they are not promptly eliminated.

If you keep these basic principles in mind, you will find it relatively easy to assign planetary rulerships to metabolic substances and processes even when a reference book does not give the proper rulership.

One other principle of astro-nutrition should be kept firmly in mind—that just because a substance is valuable to the body in proper amount, *too much of a good thing can be just as bad as the lack of it*. Too much vitamin A and D, for example, can damage the liver; too much salt can cause hypertension; too much sugar, hypoglycemia; and too much fat, obesity. For good nutrition, excesses of all kinds should be avoided.

4

PROTEINS
IN THE DIET

In this chapter we shall discuss the basic substance called protein and its vital role in the nutrition of all living things. Protein is the only known substance that is capable of what we understand to be life. The living part of all animals and plants is composed of protein. In the process of living, the protein in animal and plant cells wears out and must be continually replaced if the organism is to stay alive. Plants manufacture protein from amino acids, which in turn are manufactured from the minerals taken in from the soil through their roots. Animals obtain their protein by eating either plants or other animals. Animals that obtain their protein strictly from plant sources are called *herbivores*, as for example the cow or the termite. Animals like the lion and the eagle that derive their protein solely from other animals are called *carnivores*. Those, like man, that derive their protein from both sources are called *omnivores*.

Protein is not a single chemical compound; it is the name given to a class of compounds, all of which are composed of carbon, hydrogen, oxygen, nitrogen and sulfur. A single protein molecule is large in comparison to most other chemical molecules and extremely complex, containing hundreds of atoms of each of the five elements listed above. Only recently, by using highly sophisticated electronic instruments, have scientists begun to unlock the secrets of the protein molecule.

Because of the complex structure of protein, astrologers have never been able to fully agree as to its sign or planetary rulership. In this chapter I will attempt to establish what I believe to be the astrological rulership of protein. But to do this and to understand more clearly what protein is and why it is essential, we must start at the beginning—how the body constructs its own protein.

Composition of Proteins

The body constructs protein from very simple building blocks called amino acids. Just as words and sentences are made of letters, the body builds protein from amino acids. Coincidentally, there are twenty-six letters in our alphabet and about twenty-six amino acids. Ten or fifteen more are known, but their functions are not well understood. And just as each group of people constructs its own language, each species constructs its own brand of protein. For example, while beef and pork are both basically protein, they taste different because they are not the same kind of protein. Each animal puts the amino acid building blocks together in a variety of different ways that are characteristic of the species.

Fundamental to any understanding of nutrition and digestion is an understanding of how each living organism manufactures its own protein from the amino acids. To begin with, the body gets amino acids from the protein foods we eat. However, we cannot absorb this protein directly, first, because it is insoluble in water, and second, because the combination of amino acids is foreign to the body's protein. The protein we eat must first be broken down into its amino acid components (which are water soluble and thus digestible) and then reassembled in the body cells to form proteins that are characteristic of the human species and of our own particular hereditary pattern. No two humans are exactly alike, and our body rejects protein that is foreign to its hereditary pattern. This is why transplanting organs from one body to another has been so difficult, except in twins of very similar heredity.

In the first stages of protein digestion, which occur in the stomach, the protein we eat is broken down into its components by stomach acid and various digestive enzymes like pepsin. The enzymes continue this process in the small intestine. Unlike protein, the amino acids are water soluble and thus can be absorbed into the body through the wall of the small intestine.

The breaking down of protein into amino acids is a Mars process, since in astro-nutritional theory Mars always symbolizes processes that break down complex compounds into simpler ones. Like all acids, the amino acids are ruled by Mars. The reassembling of these acids into body protein is a Venus process, since Venus symbolizes the synthesis of simpler substances into those that are more complex. Mars and Venus traditionally represent opposites in astrology.

Taking this symbolism one step further, Venus and Jupiter are always paired, as are Mars and Saturn. Jupiter symbolizes the end product of Venus processes; Saturn, the end product of Mars processes. Thus, we see why Jupiter rules fat and weight gain, while Saturn rules feces and weight loss. The body stores Jupiter substances and seeks to eliminate Saturn waste products. Carbon dioxide, the waste product of respiration, is Saturn ruled.

Pluto, which symbolically represents heredity and all processes of replication, ultimately controls the replication of worn-out protein by new protein. It rules the cell's nucleus, which contains the hereditary material that is the template on which the amino acids are reassembled to form new protein. When something happens to this Plutonian template, the metabolism of the cell goes awry and we have a cancer cell, which accounts for Pluto's rulership over cancerous growths and tumors.

Do not infer from this discussion that Saturn processes are all "bad" and Jupiter processes all "good." It's about time we eliminated these good and bad tags in astrology. It is good that the body eliminates that which it does not need, and it is bad when we acquire too much Jupiterian fat! Saturn checks the excesses of Jupiter.

To what planet then shall we assign the rulership of protein, the only chemical substance capable of life? For the answer to this question we have to look at the planetary exaltations. What planet is exalted in the Venus-ruled signs of Taurus and Libra? The Moon is exalted in Taurus, but we already know that the Moon rules all the body fluids. Thus, it is Saturn, exalted in Libra, that rules protein. Saturn, together with the Moon, ultimately determines the body's form and shape, including the skeleton, which is also Saturn ruled. Saturn, then, is exalted in Libra, Venus' sign, while Mars is exalted in Capricorn, Saturn's sign. Saturn ties the Venusian and Martian processes together in an order that makes sense.

The Sun rules the body's vital heat-forming processes. Its opposite, the Moon, puts out the fire, in that water dilutes and slows down the heat-forming process, and perspiration cools the body. Jupiter, which is exalted in Cancer, rules fat, which also slows down physical activity and dampens the metabolism of sugar (glucose), which is an essential ingredient in producing energy.

We cannot understand the process of metabolism and nutrition properly if we hang on to the "good" and "bad" connotations given to Jupiter and Saturn by earlier astrologers.

The Amino Acids

We have learned how the process of digestion breaks down the complex protein molecule into its component amino acids. These are later reassembled in the cells to produce human protein, a process that is similar to stringing a number of colored beads according to a particular sequence.

All but eight of the amino acids are considered to be nonessential, because the body can synthesize them from other amino acids. If a nonessential amino acid is missing in the diet, the human body can manufacture it. The remaining eight amino acids are indispensible, because the body cannot synthesize or manufacture them. A deficiency of one or more of these essential amino acids in the diet soon has extremely harmful effects upon the body. Some of these effects are:

> Lowered blood pressure
> Poor digestion and constipation
> Fatigue, lack of endurance
> Bones that fracture more easily
> Excessive water retention in tissues
> Wounds that heal poorly or fail to heal
> Weakened hair and nails
> Lowered resistance to infection
> Anemia
> Loss of muscle tone

Unless we eat foods or combinations of foods that contain adequate amounts of all the essential proteins, normal body functions are impaired. Unfortunately, the foods that have these essential amino acids are the most expensive. While we get protein from both animal and plant sources, *no single plant protein supplies all of these essential amino acids in sufficient amounts*, not even soybeans. Vegetarians, please take heed!

Foods that contain proper amounts of the essential amino acids include dairy products like milk and cheese, meat, fish, poultry and eggs. Certain plant proteins, such as those in soybeans, nuts, yeast and wheat germ do contain all of the amino acids, but the quantities of the essential amino acids in an ordinary serving are inadequate to fulfill daily nutritional requirements. However, they are rich in other essentials and have an important place in your diet. Thus, if you choose not to eat meat, be sure that your diet contains plenty of eggs and dairy products. Grain products and legumes (peas and beans) are also sources of plant protein, but they lack one or more of the essential amino acids. Mushrooms are the only plant food that comes close to supplying enough of the essential amino acids.

Neptune and Your Diet

The average adult male weighing 155 pounds requires about 70 grams of protein per day; the average adult female weighing 125 pounds requires about 60 grams (100 grams while nursing a baby). Protein foods also have calories. Many people on a diet, unless they plan carefully, may get less than the minimum daily requirement of protein while cutting back on the calories.

A good, carefully planned diet can accomplish wonders, but an inadequately planned diet, including many of the current fad diets, can be disastrous. Virgo represents nutrition and good diet. Neptune represents our ideal of the slim, trim body, but Neptune also represents deceit—and it is in its detriment in Virgo! Many people who are now in their forties were born with Neptune in Virgo, and this is the age group that is particularly attracted to fad diets, since they are losing their youthful figures and bodies. Don't let Neptune pull the wool over your eyes and deceive you—now you know better. Oh, you say, my Neptune is in Leo (if you're in your fifties) or in Libra (if you're in your thirties or late twenties). Do I have the same problem? When it comes to diet and the proper selection of foods, we *all* have a problem with Neptune. However, this problem is especially characteristic of the generation with Neptune in Virgo, who are so inclined to excesses of junk food.

Neptune in general represents chemical substances that we ingest that are not meant to be part of a normal healthy diet. Neptune symbolizes drugs of all sorts, nicotine, alcohol and many other poisonous substances. These Neptune compounds are both subtle and deceptive in the true astrological manner, for most of them simulate natural substances that the body needs.

A few common examples illustrate this point beautifully. Caffeine in coffee simulates adrenalin in its effect upon the body—it stimulates the release of glucose and speeds up the metabolic rate. Alcohol simulates glucose, and it is now believed that the body actually prefers alcohol to glucose in the basic process of oxidation, for alcohol too will produce energy and calories. A simple drug like aspirin turns off pain, but pain is a symptom, a warning, that something is wrong in that area of the body. When you turn off the pain with aspirin, you are lulled into a false sense of security that whatever was wrong has gone away. Food additives "trick" us into seeing our food in other than its true natural state. Artificial sweeteners trick our taste buds into thinking something is sweet, when of course it is not and may well contain no sugar at all.

The golden rule of the nutritional astrologer ought to be: "Beware of Neptune and all the foods and substances that it rules." Most of these substances are harmful to the body in some way. Poisons, ruled by both Pluto and Neptune, are substances that interfere with and often destroy some essential body process. Plutonian poisons and their sources are easily recognized, like venomous snakes and lizards, scorpions or poisonous mushrooms. Neptunian poisons are subtle and not easily recognized.

The most insidious poisons of all, however, are those that interfere with protein metabolism, such as plant alkaloids (heroin, cocaine) and heavy metals (lead). Neptune is in its fall in Capricorn, ruled by Saturn, which also rules protein. No one now living has Neptune in Capricorn in their chart, but planets in Capricorn aspecting Neptune sometimes have this effect. And in the 1980's, Neptune will again be in Capricorn. Those who now saturate their diets with Neptunian substances may reap the reward of this body abuse at that time.

However, Neptune is in its exaltation in Cancer, which is ruled by the Moon, the natural astrological antidote for Neptune illnesses and problems. This is because the Moon rules water—pure, simple water, which dilutes and washes away many poisonous substances. Urine is nothing more than a complex solution of substances that would in time poison the body if they were not regularly eliminated. Urea, the principal component of urine, is the end product of protein metabolism, the form in which used-up protein is eliminated from the body. Urea is probably ruled by Saturn, but urine is ruled by Pluto and Scorpio (the eliminative function). Urine also eliminates excess salt and sugars when their concentration in the body rises above healthy levels. Normally the urine contains salt and trace amounts of sugar. Noted nutritionists, including Carlton Fredericks, claim that sugars and excessive salt in the diet constitute the greatest threat to life and longevity in the United States. The fact that the body recognizes excess amounts of these substances as poisons (Pluto rules the urine and its contents) lends astrological credence to Fredericks' theory.

To sum up, protein, ruled by Saturn, is the only chemical substance we know of that is capable of life. Its building blocks are amino acids, ruled by Mars. Adequate amounts of the eight essential amino acids are a must *every day* as part of a nutritionally sound diet. Neptune-ruled substances, on the other hand, should be eliminated as much as possible from the body and diet. Since it is almost impossible to completely eliminate these substances, pure water should be included in the diet in sufficient quantity to dilute and wash them out of the body in the urine. Today, the only pure water is distilled water, because pollution has affected all water sources, even high mountain springs.

5

CARBOHYDRATES
AND METABOLISM

In this chapter we examine the important role of carbohydrates in the nutrition of the body. We discuss how the body cells get their energy, why they must have energy and how the digestive process provides the material to produce this energy. We also discuss the roles of Venus and Jupiter, Mars and Saturn in producing and using energy and how the body provides for an energy reserve or stockpile of fuel that can be used when the body is under stress. All carbohydrates, including sugars and starches, are under the rulership of Venus.

The Vital Role of Glucose

One of the primary goals of the digestive process is to provide every body cell with sufficient amounts of energy to sustain itself and remain alive. Many of the vital chemical reactions that take place in the cell require energy, which is derived from the oxidation of the simple sugar, glucose, within the cell. Glucose is carried to the cell as the end product of carbohydrate metabolism. There, in the presence of enzymes and oxygen, the glucose is converted into carbon dioxide, water and energy. The carbon dioxide and water are nonessential by-products of this reaction; the important product is the heat energy, which is derived from the glucose.

glucose + oxygen ———▶ carbon dioxide + water + heat
      (enzyme)   energy

The oxygen used in this chemical reaction is brought from the lungs to the cell by the red corpuscles, containing hemoglobin, in the blood. The hemoglobin and oxygen combine chemically until enzymes in the cell separate them for use in oxidation. Note the importance of the cell enzymes in this whole process.

Glucose is one of literally hundreds of chemical compounds called carbohydrates or saccharides. The molecules of all carbohydrates are made up of building blocks called simple sugars. Carbohydrates may be subdivided into three groups, namely:

Monosaccharides, like glucose, consist of a *single* sugar building block.

Disaccharides, like common table sugar (sucrose) consist of *two* simple sugarbuilding blocks.

Polysaccharides, like starch and cellulose, consist of *many* simple sugar building blocks joined together in a long line in daisy-chain fashion.

It appears that the only carbohydrate of any chemical value to the body is the simple sugar or monosaccharide called *glucose.* Therefore, one of the major goals of the digestive process is to extract the glucose from the various carbohydrates that we ingest every day.

Diet watchers count their calories, but what is a calorie? It is a measurement of heat energy and is equivalent to the amount of heat required to raise the temperature of one liter of water one degree Centigrade or nearly two degrees Fahrenheit. For every gram of glucose that the body oxidizes, 3.74 calories of heat are produced, enough to raise the temperature of a liter of water about 6½ degrees F. When more glucose is produced than the body needs for its immediate requirements, the glucose is stored in various forms in the body—the most obvious form being fat. A proper diet should include sufficient energy foods to meet the body's needs, plus a slight excess for storage purposes. Thus, when you count calories, you are actually measuring the amount of energy that your body is receiving through the process of digestion.

Storage and Release of Energy

The demand for energy varies with the amount of activity being carried on by the body. Therefore it is essential that there be some means for storing or stockpiling energy to meet demand during peak periods of activity or stress. The first means of stockpiling is to temporarily convert glucose back to a polysaccharide or starch form. Both animals and plants do this.

The reverse of the body's glucose oxidation process takes place in the leaves of every plant in photosynthesis, in which carbon dioxide from the air is combined with water from the earth to form glucose, which is stored by the plant as starch. Photosynthesis takes place only in sunlight and thus is a chemical process for storing up solar energy. But the plant uses energy at night also, and thus the starch is the plant's glucose reserve source.

The human body does something similar. It stores excess glucose in the form of animal starch, called glycogen, in the liver and muscle tissue. But there is a limit to the amount of glycogen the body can produce and store—about 500 milligrams. After that, the extra glucose is converted to fat. Glycogen is ruled by Jupiter, as is fat.

Unlike plants, which remain stationary, animals move about and thus experience more stressful situations and crises, when added glucose energy is required very suddenly. When such an emergency occurs, the body signals the need for added energy by releasing the hormone *adrenalin* (ruled by Mars) into the bloodstream. Adrenalin quickly breaks down the glycogen molecules into glucose, providing added energy to deal with the emergency situation.

Shortly after eating a meal, the body is flooded with far more glucose than it could use, were it not for the liver and muscle, where the excess glucose is stored as glycogen. Later, between meals, as the supply of glucose in the bloodstream is slowly used up, another hormone called cortin (also Mars ruled) triggers the slow conversion of glycogen back into glucose.

glycogen + cortin = glucose (proceeds slowly)
glycogen + adrenalin = glucose (proceeds rapidly)

One symptom of lowered blood sugar level is sleepiness or tiredness. Another is hunger. Tired automobile drivers are urged to stop for a cup of strong coffee, which contains the drug caffeine, in order to stay awake at the wheel. Caffeine, ruled by Neptune, is similar in chemical nature and structure to adrenalin, and when it gets into the bloodstream it tricks the body into converting glycogen back to glucose in much the same way that adrenalin does. Thus, the driver wakes up again and becomes more alert for a brief time.

glycogen + caffeine = glucose (proceeds rapidly)

This is why caffeine is considered to be a stimulant. It stimulates the release of glucose, raising the blood sugar level temporarily, which is why some people find it difficult to sleep at night after drinking coffee. The strength of the caffeine effect depends upon how sensitive Neptune is in your chart. For example, a person with Neptune in an angular house is more sensitive to this effect than a person whose Neptune is cadent. But it is those with Neptune in succedent houses and fixed signs who generally cannot sleep, because the caffeine effect is fixed and therefore more prolonged.

The conversion of glucose to glycogen for temporary storage and later release as needed is promoted by the hormone insulin. Diabetics, whose bodies do not produce enough insulin, lack the ability to properly store glucose as glycogen. Because glucose is not converted to glycogen, the blood sugar level goes way above normal, until the kidneys, in trying to protect the body from sugar crystallization in the blood, start to excrete sugar as glucose in the urine.

The opposite of diabetes, hypoglycemia or low blood sugar, is apparently much more common, according to Carlton Fredericks and other nutritionists. In this condition the body produces *too much* insulin, to the point that so much glucose is stored as glycogen that there is not enough glucose in the bloodstream to maintain normal body function. The person feels persistently tired and listless from lack of sufficient energy for normal body processes. If early research findings are confirmed, hypoglycemia may well be a root cause of such problems as asthma, alcoholism, rheumatic heart disease, varicose veins and a variety of other conditions whose exact cause is not completely understood. It is interesting to note that asthmatics rarely have diabetes, and that if they do contract it, the symptoms of asthma seem to magically disappear!

Glycogen, ruled by Jupiter, is the end product of a reaction that starts with Venus-ruled glucose. Thus we can say that the sugar storage process is a Venus-Jupiter function, with Jupiter representing the end product. The burning or destruction of glucose is ruled by Mars, and the end product of its destruction, carbon dioxide, is ruled by Saturn.

This illustrates a very important principle of nutritional astrology, that Venus and Jupiter together represent the building-up or growth processes. Mars and Saturn together represent the destructive or aging processes. When you reach the late twenties, these Mars-Saturn processes become dominant, and the body begins to slowly break down as aging proceeds. Thus the goal of proper nutrition is to retard the Mars-Saturn aging effect as long as possible. Venus triggers the growth process, the end result of which is Jupiter. That is why Jupiter represents growth in traditional astrological symbolism. Mars triggers the aging process, and Saturn, the "grim reaper," represents the end product—breakdown. This also explains why the Venus-Jupiter ruled vitamins and minerals become so important in your later years. Persons with an afflicted Saturn or Mars require larger amounts of these vitamins and minerals in their diet than the average person.

Now you can readily see how Jupiter, representing too much of a good thing, is so involved in obesity. Jupiter rules fat, the product of too much Venus activity or sugar intake. Also this is why fat people tend to retain too much fluid in their body—the Moon rules body fluids, and Jupiter is exalted in Cancer. And those with Sagittarius rising (Jupiter-ruled persons) tend to be taller than people with other rising signs.

On the other hand, Saturn is exalted in Libra, indicating that a "well-balanced" diet is the best defense against Saturn's aging process. Mars is exalted in Capricorn, which is Saturn's sign. When Mars is in this sign, it is kept under control, and the aging process proceeds more slowly. People with Mars in Capricorn or Saturn in Libra often look younger than they are.

Carbohydrate Digestion

We are ready now to see how the body chemically derives glucose from the carbohydrates in the diet and how this process is influenced by natal planetary positions. Let us take as our example a slice of bread, a food rich in carbohydrates. Before wheat is milled, the starch in the kernels is enclosed in microscopic sacs or casings composed of cellulose. Although cellulose is a carbohydrate, it is indigestible by human beings. (Paper and wood fiber are cellulose, and if the body could digest cellulose, the paper on which this page is printed would be digestible.) Milling removes the cellulose casings, making the wheat starch more digestible, but it also removes valuable vitamins and minerals that are in the casings.

As a general rule, the longer the chain of glucose molecules within the starch molecule, the harder the starch is to digest. Thus we do certain things to the starch molecule to shorten its length. Heat shortens the molecules, so we bake our bread. Toasting the bread carries this process further, by breaking the starch molecule down into a brown compound called dextran. Dextran is the crust on a loaf of bread and the golden-brown coating on toast. It too is a polysaccharide, but its chain length is greatly shortened, making it much more digestible. That is why a sick person is often given toast.

Carbohydrate digestion begins with food preparation, as do all digestive processes, sometimes long before we eat the food. This explains why we prepare certain foods in special ways before eating it.

When you take a bite of your slice of bread, enzymes in the saliva as you chew begin to chop the long-chain carbohydrate molecule down into smaller molecules of maltose, a disaccharide. The longer you chew each mouthful, the more carbohydrate is broken down. Note also that the longer you chew the bread, the sweeter it tastes, because maltose, which is Venus-ruled, is a sugar.

After the bread is swallowed, it enters the stomach, where hydrochloric acid in the digestive juices quickly completes the breakdown process. The remaining starch and maltose are broken down further into glucose, ready for immediate digestion. Athletes often eat foods rich in dextrose (another name for glucose) just before a game, because this gives them plenty of reserve energy that does not have to be digested. The dextrose in a candy bar provides this vital energy. Table sugar, which is sucrose, a disaccharide, is also readily digestible, because it contains a glucose molecule. But if this energy source is not rapidly used up in vigorous bodily exercise, it gets stored first as glycogen and then as fat. This explains why a high-carbohydrate diet is used for weight gain and why the intake of carbohydrates must be carefully controlled in order to lose weight.

For the average person, 60 grams of carbohydrate a day is sufficient to maintain body weight; 30 grams of carbohydrate will result in the loss of about one pound per day, while 90 grams will increase the weight by about one pound per day. The low-carbohydrate diet that is becoming popular is based on this principle. Starving people usually have a diet of less than 30 grams of carbohydrate per day, a strict regimen that is not recommended. On the other hand, every added pound of fat adds about three miles of capillaries to the blood vascular system. Pumping blood through these capillaries naturally places added strain on the heart, which is why overweight people tend to have higher blood pressure and are in greater danger of injury to the heart and blood circulation.

During Jupiter transits of your first house, which represents the physical body as a whole, the tendency is to overeat and thus gain weight. This occurs about once every twelve years, and it is an important time to watch your diet carefully. On the other hand, a Saturn transit of the first house is an ideal time to lose weight, since Saturn restricts gain during the two or three years it takes to transit this house.

Fiber in the Diet

No discussion of carbohydrates would be complete without mentioning the need for fiber, or cellulose, in the daily diet, even though fiber has no recognized nutritional value! The human body cannot digest cellulose, even though it has the same basic chemical formula as starch—with one important exception. If we could magnify a cellulose molecule and a starch molecule, we would see that they are mirror images of each other. The body recognizes this difference, and it has no enzymes that can break down the cellulose molecule. Certain animals, such as cows, can break down cellulose, as can termites, which live on wood, also largely cellulose.

The astrological rulership for cellulose has never been clearly established, but I believe that it is Jupiter since, like fat and glycogen, it is the end product of carbohydrate metabolism in plants. Cellulose is strictly a plant product.

Scientists and nutritionists prefix the letters "d-" and "l-" to the names of chemicals that have this mirror-image property. Besides the carbohydrates, the molecules of amino acids and many vitamins also have this property. In almost all cases, human enzymes recognize and use the d-form but cannot do anything with the l-form. Compounds manufactured synthetically are a mixture of both forms and are thus labeled "dl- ." In buying vitamins, you should check the formula very carefully, because the body can utilize only the "d-" form; all of the "l-" form passes through the digestive tract unused. Louis Pasteur is credited with this discovery.

Most of what we refer to as fiber or roughage is cellulose, an "l-" form carbohydrate, and the average American diet tends to be low in roughage. The idea that roughage is necessary in the diet used to be considered an old wives' tale, but a mounting body of evidence now suggests that fiber can be an important defense against rectal and intestinal cancer and a host of related problems of the intestinal tract. After lung cancer, cancer of the rectum and colon are the most common forms of cancer today in the United States. During 1977 they will strike nearly 100,000 Americans (slightly more than 4 per 10,000 population), and nearly half will die as a result. Yet in underdeveloped countries, where people eat mostly the cheaper forms of carbohydrates, which are relatively unrefined and thus high in fiber, the incidence of this form of cancer is slightly less than 4 per 100,000 population. Also these people rarely become obese.

People whose diet is high in fiber (between 20 and 25 grams daily) also have a very low rate of appendicitis. The function of fiber is that it helps food pass through the intestine more quickly. Certain bacteria in the intestine, which is a veritable treasure-trove of bacteria, both helpful and harmful, act on the bile salts to form compounds that are known as carcinogens (substances that cause cancer). The longer it takes material to travel through the intestinal tract, the more time these carcinogens have to work their sabotage. Insufficient fiber in the diet also may be a major cause of constipation, intestinal growths called polyps and even heart disease, because of increased cholesterol levels in the blood.

Foods high in fiber include whole-wheat bread, unrefined

flour, broccoli, Brussels sprouts, cauliflower, beets, carrots, potato skins and most leafy vegetables. The richest source is bran, which is part of wheat germ. Bran flour, now available in any health-food store, is excellent for breading meats and vegetables before cooking, and when mixed with seasoning, it is a great flavor enhancer. Breakfast cereals that have the word bran in their name are usually high in fiber content, which is often indicated on the box. If you use these cereals to increase your daily fiber intake, however, avoid the presweetened brands and sweeten your cereal with honey instead of sugar. Honey is much more healthful, because it contains other nutritious substances in addition to sugar.

A Word About Alcohol

We usually think of alcohol as a rather volatile liquid that burns when lighted and has a characteristic odor. Wood alcohol (methyl alcohol) and grain alcohol (ethyl alcohol) are typical examples. The chemist, however, knows that most alcohols are not liquid at all, but white crystalline solids. Although sugar is a form of alcohol, its molecule is much more complex than that of grain alcohol. Sorry about that, all of you teetotalers who put sugar in your tea or coffee. You can become just as addicted to sugar as to alcohol, especially if Venus (sugar) is closely conjunct the Moon (your habit patterns) in your natal chart or if you have a Moon-Venus sextile or trine. Have you noticed that most of the "cures" for alcoholism involve substituting sweets for alcohol and that eating a large amount of sugar kills your desire for alcohol? You are merely substituting one kind of alcohol for another!

The interesting thing about ethyl alcohol, which is the alcoholic constituent of all intoxicating drinks, is that the body will use it as an energy supply in preference to glucose. As far as we know, glucose can be absorbed only through the walls of the small intestine, but ethyl alcohol is absorbed right through the stomach walls before it even gets to the small intestine. Ethyl

72

alcohol needs no digestion at all; the body takes it in very quickly as it is. And what is even more important, the cells burn the alcohol just like glucose.

The problem, in part, stems from the fact that excess alcohol destroys protein, especially the protein that constitutes nerve fibers. The brain is rich in nerve fibers, and too much alcohol destroys these fibers and thus the sensory functions, resulting in impaired motor nerve responses.

Thanks to Mother Nature and thousands of years of evolution, during which man naturally ingested vegetable material in various states of fermentation, which produces grain alcohol, the body developed a natural defense against abnormal amounts of this "poison." A special liver enzyme, ethylase, has the sole and specific function of converting ethyl alcohol into carbon dioxide and water before it can injure the body. The material from which the body constructs ethylase is thiamine or vitamin B-1, which is a valuable constituent of all common hangover remedies. Normally the body contains enough ethylase to convert about one shot of alcohol per hour into carbon dioxide and water without any deleterious effects—that is, drunkenness. More rapid consumption of alcohol overpowers this enzyme, and the normal signs of drunkenness begin to appear as the alcohol affects the motor nerve responses.

As one might expect, ethyl alcohol is ruled by Neptune. Alcohol is deceptive because the body cannot distinguish between glucose and ethyl alcohol when it is present in excessive quantity. Only the liver, co-ruled by Neptune (the body's defensive processes), can detect the difference and convert this poison to inoffensive by-products.

For methyl alcohol, the body has no defensive enzymes. Ingesting any quantity of wood alcohol quickly results in the denaturing of the body protein and rapid death.

As astrologers, let us recognize in symbolic terms the results of alcohol ingestion. Neptune substances such as alcohol deceive the body into unnatural responses. When someone rationalizes that he or she is a moderate drinker, one must ask,

"How moderate? How much alcohol is consumed per hour? More than one ounce? Two ounces? Five?" When someone says that Scotch is less intoxicating (or fattening) than bourbon or beer, the question that must be asked is: "Why is it necessary to drink alcohol in the first place?" To supply energy that is not being supplied from natural glucose sources? To escape from the frustrations of life?

Many astrologers are interested in the problems that lead to excessive alcohol comsumption and alcoholism, which society has come to recognize as a disease. No one has yet established a "signature" of alcoholism based upon the symbolism of the natal horoscope. However, one can certainly assume that Venus, representing sugar metabolism; Neptune, because alcohol is a sugar substitute and a deceiver of the metabolism; and the Moon, our habit patterns, must be involved in the problems of the alcoholic.

In this chapter I have tried to explain what carbohydrates and sugars are. We have seen that the digestive process must reduce carbohydrate molecules to glucose, which is the fuel that each cell uses in all the other chemical reactions that keep the cell alive. The process of breaking down the complex carbohydrates is ruled by Mars and Saturn (analysis). The body stores glucose for times when it needs extra energy. The storage of glucose, first as glycogen (animal starch), with the excess stored as fat, is a Venus-Jupiter (synthesis) process.

Each step of the breaking-down and building-up process is controlled by body enzymes or hormones. When an enzyme or hormone, for example, insulin, is lacking or in insufficient supply, normal metabolism of sugar is disrupted, and a disease condition results: in this case, diabetes. On the other hand, too much of a hormone can also result in a chemical imbalance and disease; too much insulin causes hypoglycemia.

Neptune-ruled substances, like caffeine and alcohol, closely resemble normal chemicals needed in nutrition and "trick" the body into false responses, thus causing the body to react in unnatural ways.

6

FATS IN
THE DIET

In our present-day American culture, the word "fat" has a rather bad name; in fact, to certain food faddists it is a dirty four-letter word! However, fat does play a very important—yes, even vital—role in our daily diet. We cannot live without a certain amount of fat, and it would be virtually impossible to eliminate it from the normal American diet. In fact, when we do not get certain fatty substances in our diet every day, the body synthesizes them from other food that we eat.

It is important that anyone seriously interested in good nutrition learn to take a balanced and sensible view about fats. It is also important that anyone in astrology who wishes to clearly understand the full range of astro-nutritional symbolism take a balanced and intelligent view of this controversial subject.

Composition of Fats

In general terms, we all know what fat is. It can be that unsightly bulge as we approach middle age, especially the flabby tissue that builds up at the hips and waistline. Fat is also that greasy substance that collects in the pan when we fry or roast meat. Butter and lard are fats that come from animal sources, and margarine is fat derived from plant sources. As far as we know, all plants and animals produce and utilize fat in their metabolism.

During the Second World War, you may recall that homemakers did their patriotic duty by saving fats of all kinds and returning them to their butchers, for which they were paid several cents per pound. Not many people remember why, however. Those of you in the Pluto in Gemini generation may remember that on the farm, fats were saved for making old-fashioned lye soap. The fats were mixed with lye, made from wood ashes, in a special iron kettle, boiled to make the lye and fat react, and finally the soap was skimmed off.

Chemically, soap is a combination of a metallic mineral such as sodium or potassium, which comes from the lye, and a fatty acid, which comes from the fat. The soap makers are concerned only with this product; they are not concerned with what remains in the pot after the soap has been removed. During the Second World War, however, the principal concern was with a chemical called glycerin, the constituent of the fat molecule that remains in the soap kettle. Glycerin has many commercial uses. When treated with nitric acid, it is converted into nitroglycerin, from which dynamite and other explosives are manufactured. Alfred Nobel invented the process for converting nitroglycerin into dynamite, which, as we might expect, is ruled by Uranus.

Thus, the first important fact to learn about fat is that its molecule consists of a fatty acid linked to glycerin. Astrologically, Jupiter is the ruler of fats, so we can assume that they have an important part in the growth process. Like all acids, fatty acids are ruled by Mars, and glycerin, like all alcohols, is ruled by Neptune. Mars with Neptune is not a happy astrological combination. Mars is exalted in Capricorn; Neptune is in its fall in this sign. Neptune is generally considered to be exalted in Cancer; Mars is in its fall in Cancer. Remembering that the Cancer–Capricorn sign pair is physiologically concerned with protection and containment, we gain a new insight into the function of fats. Fats provide a reserve source of energy, *containing* this energy within the body. Thus, fats *protect* the body from excessive heat loss. Those ancient astrologers may not have been very good biochemists (or were they?), but they certainly had a good grasp of bio-astrology.

We can see that fatty substances have a potential for energy (Mars) and also a potential for toxicity (Neptune). When the body burns fats, these toxins are removed by water. Neptune is exalted in Cancer, the Moon's sign, and the Moon rules body fluids, including water. Mars is exalted in Capricorn, ruled by Saturn, which rules carbon dioxide, the by-product of burning fat for energy. I never cease to be impressed with how beautifully the symbolism of astrology and the symbolism of chemistry fit together!

Saturated and Unsaturated Fats

Magazines today are full of articles on health and diet. Often these articles mention *saturated* and *unsaturated* fats. What do these terms mean? Why are unsaturated fats particularly important in the diet, and why have saturated fats gotten such a bad name?

In the first place, fat comes in two forms, liquid and solid. As a general rule, animal fats are solid and vegetable fats are liquid at room temperature. Fats that are solid at room temperature, like Crisco and bacon fat, are for the most part saturated fats. Fats that are liquid at room temperature, like olive oil or corn oil, are of the unsaturated variety.

A famous brand of peanut butter was recently advertised as having the "stalemakers" removed to enhance its flavor. What does that mean? A molecule of saturated fat contains all of the hydrogen atoms it can hold, while molecules of unsaturated fat can take on other atoms from the environment. When they take on oxygen atoms from the air, these fats become rancid. So the manufacturers add hydrogen to the unsaturated peanut oil so that it won't take on oxygen and become rancid. Smart? Perhaps. The problem is that while the hydrogenated peanut butter may be pleasing to the palate, it is less digestible, because the body can digest unsaturated fats much more easily than fats that are saturated. Thus, anything that has been hydrogenated has been saturated with hydrogen, but in the process made less digestible.

Another important fact about hydrogenation is that it requires a metal catalyst, such as nickel or platinum. There has always been some question whether all of this metal is removed from the food or whether it has been eliminated to "acceptable levels." As you will see in the next chapter, catalysts are ruled by Pluto, and Plutonian substances can be toxic to the body.

The body requires a certain amount of unsaturated fat on a daily basis for good nutrition. Because unsaturated fats are far more chemically active than saturated fats, they provide the raw materials for many more nutrients and chemical reactions. If you eliminate fats from your pet's diet, the fur becomes dry and falls out more freely. If you eliminate them from your own diet, the consequences are similar, although more subtle, as I will explain.

For the moment let us assume that you are already conscious of the need for unsaturated fats and therefore have chosen to use unsaturated margarine instead of saturated butter. You store this fat at a cool temperature so that it does not oxidize, or turn rancid. (Rancidity, incidentally, is also ruled by Pluto). Are you improving your nutrition by using unsaturated fats? Not necessarily, unless your diet contains sufficient amounts of vitamin C and vitamin E! Both of these vitamins are termed "antioxidants," that is, they prevent unsaturated fats from turning into saturated fats. During the digestive process, unsaturated fats can become saturated with oxygen molecules unless there is some antioxidant present to prevent this.

Cholesterol—Friend or Foe?

Lately, cholesterol has had far too much negative publicity in the popular literature. I think it is high time that we add some *sense* to a lot of this *nonsense*. When I was studying biochemistry in college, a professor of mine told us that back in the 1920's he had decided to eliminate cholesterol from his diet, because he suspected, even then, that it contributed to heart disease. His study showed that about the only food he could consume that had no cholesterol in it was a martini—provided he threw away the olive, which is rich in cholesterol.

Closely related to the fats is the class of chemical compounds called sterols or fatty alcohols, to which cholesterol belongs. Researchers have long suspected that excessive cholesterol buildup on the walls of the arteries contributes to heart attack, the medical term for which is myocardial infarction. What happens is that a cholesterol plaque breaks free from the wall of the artery and is carried to the heart region, where it blocks off the flow of blood into the coronary artery, which feeds the heart. Cholesterol is also thought to contribute to so-called hardening of the arteries in old age.

Many individuals have made some rather passionate attempts to cut down and even eliminate cholesterol from their diets. However, I'm afraid that they are fighting a losing battle, as my professor discovered. It is impossible to completely eliminate cholesterol from the diet, and it is not good to try. Cholesterol is so important to nutrition that if the body does not get it on a daily basis, it synthesizes it from other food substances called triglycerides. The body normally requires about 2 grams, or 2000 milligrams, of cholesterol daily. The problem is that some people, because of their genetic makeup, manufacture, or synthesize, more than 2 grams, which causes problems. Pluto, ruler of the genetic makeup of the body, is the culprit here.

When the body has to synthesize cholesterol, it uses saturated fats in preference to unsaturated fats, for which the body has more important uses. Thus, if saturated fats are completely eliminated from the diet, unsaturated fats are used and subverted from their primary use. And, as you might imagine, this can cause problems, unless the diet is rich in unsaturated fats.

Eggs are the richest natural source of cholesterol, specifically the yolk. The natural biological function of the egg is to produce a chicken. If cholesterol is "bad" for the living organism, why does nature provide the chicken embryo with so much cholesterol? It is a source of energy to the developing chick. As the embryo develops, it converts the cholesterol into energy (a

Mars process), eventually destroying the egg. And to what planet do we assign the rulership of eggs? Venus, of course, the antithesis of Mars. Venus builds, Mars destroys. An egg contains approximately 700 milligrams of cholesterol, so you can eat several eggs per day if other sources of cholesterol are diminished.

Why does the body manufacture cholesterol if it is not supplied from the diet? For a very important reason. Cholesterol is a vital raw material from which the body manufactures certain life-giving compounds. In the presence of sunlight on the skin, the body uses cholesterol to manufacture Vitamin D, or ergosterol, which is another sterol. Cholesterol is used to manufacture the bile salts, which metabolize other fats, and cholesterol is used by the adrenal glands and sex organs to manufacture the sex hormones, which are also sterols.

Vitamin D is ruled by the Sun; in fact, it is called the sunshine vitamin. The male sex hormones are ruled by Mars, and the female hormones by Venus. The male hormones have an inhibitory effect upon the female hormones, and vice versa, so again Mars is pitted against Venus. The Sun is exalted in Aries, which is Mars' sign.

Lecithin

Another word for fat is *lipid,* and a class of fatty compounds that we cannot overlook in this discussion is the *phospholipids*—fatty substances that contain the element phosphorus. The most celebrated member of this group is lecithin, which is just now beginning to be appreciated for its role in normal nutrition.

Lecithin occurs in all unrefined foods that contain oil. Lecithin is also an inexpensive by-product of paint manufacture, which uses vegetable oils, such as linseed oil. But lecithin in the oil causes the paint to smear, so it must be removed.

Lecithin is known to chemists as an emulsifying agent,

that is, a compound that can break large fat globules into microscopic globules. This is exactly what should not happen in paint, but it must happen in the body in order to absorb fat from the digested food in the small intestine.

Lecithin and related phospholipids are important in the diet to help absorb fats and help prevent the formation of cholesterol plaques on artery walls. Lecithin keeps the fatty substances in emulsion, in microscopic particles, a form in which they can do minimal harm to the body. One or two tablespoons of lecithin taken with each meal aids in fat metabolism and helps keep cholesterol plaques from building up. Lecithin can be taken mixed with other foods, such as fruit juices, so that its undesirable taste is disguised, or in capsules. Eggs, liver, nuts, wheat and soybean oil are particularly rich in lecithin. It is important to note that most natural sources of saturated fatty acids are also rich in lecithin. Nature not only provides the materials we need but also, in the same plant package, the materials we need to digest those materials properly. However, most meats and animal foods do not contain sufficient quantities of lecithin, so we must supply it from other sources in order to metabolize animal fat. This is why vegetables should be part of a diet that is rich in animal fats, and why man is an omnivore. Animals that eat only meat have enzymes that emulsify the animal fats. The human metabolism lacks these special enzymes, and thus the emulsifier must come from plant foods.

The astrological rulership of lecithin has not been clearly established. In my opinion, it is probably Saturn. Lecithin gives form and structure to plant cells (Saturn-Capricorn). It is particularly beneficial to the skin (Saturn ruled). It restricts (Saturn) excess deposits of fats, ruled by Jupiter. Mars is exalted in Capricorn, Saturn's ruler, and lecithin is of benefit in restoring sexual powers (Mars) during the aging process.

Lecithin reportedly performs quite a number of important functions in maintaining good health, including the following:

Provides increased immunity to pneumonia.

With vitamin E, reduces a diabetic's daily requirement for insulin.

Reduces fat storage in the liver.

Increases gamma globulin in the blood, thereby increasing resistance to infection.

Increases alertness in the elderly.

Helps lower blood pressure in some people.

Helps eliminate age spots in skin.

Keeps skin younger looking and combats acne, eczema and psoriasis.

Helps rebuild damaged nerve cells, as in multiple sclerosis.

Used in Germany to restore sexual powers in men, for seminal fluid is rich in lecithin.

Distributes fats from areas where they are not needed to areas where they can be utilized—helps eliminate "stretch marks."

Aids in assimilation of oil-soluble vitamins A,D,E and F.

Extends the life span of many laboratory animals.

Helpful in malnutrition, rickets, anemia, diabetes and tuberculosis; valuable in treating hardening of the arteries and excessive cholesterol buildup.

Metabolism of Fats

The digestion of fatty substances begins when food enters the small intestine. Two important processes must take place before the fat becomes digestible and thus usable by the body. First, the fatty acids must be separated from the glycerin, which is done by the enzyme lipase in the pancreatic fluid. Second, the resulting fatty acids must be emulsified into tiny globules so they can be absorbed into the bloodstream in the small intestine, where most of the digestion of fats takes place. A substance called cholecystokinin is released in the small intestine, which signals the gall bladder to release bile. The bile contains bile salts, manufactured from cholesterol, and phospholipids, which break down the fatty acids.

Note the Virgo characteristics of fat digestion. Virgo traditionally has the ability to break things down into their component parts, to try to make perfect that which is imperfect (in terms of what the body can use), and to separate out valuable substances from useless ones—discrimination. This is one of the principal reasons why Virgo is the assigned ruler of the small intestine.

As the foregoing description indicates, it would not be a good idea to eliminate fat from the diet, because fat is essential, in proper proportion, to good nutrition. Fat layers beneath the skin prevent excessive heat loss. Oxidation of fat requires twice as much oxygen as oxidation of sugar, but when a gram of fat is oxidized, it produces twice the energy of a gram of carbohydrate or protein. Some fat deposits constitute a reserve energy supply that can be used when needed. Without this reserve you'd need to eat about twice as often to maintain the necessary energy supply. Also, it is often the fat content of foods that makes them taste so good.

Then too, certain essential unsaturated fatty acids, such as linoleic acid, cannot be manufactured by the body. When these essential fatty acids are eliminated from the diet of experimental laboratory animals, they develop scaly skin and skin lesions that will not heal. The animals bleed more easily, their growth is retarded, and they fail to reproduce. Nursing mothers do not provide their offspring with adequate nutrition. Kidney function is severely impaired. And if essential fatty acids are withheld for a long enough time, the animals inevitably die.

Rancid fat does considerable harm by lessening the body's ability to absorb vitamins A, E and the B complex. Feeding rancid fat to lab animals produces the classical symptoms of deficiency of these vitamins. As we've pointed out, rancidity results from oxidation of fats. The higher the temperature, the more quickly oxidation takes place. When fat is fried, oxidation takes place quite rapidly, so eating large quantities of fried food means greater intake of rancid fats, which results in poor nutrition. The only value of deep frying foods, like potatoes, is that it preserves the essential vitamins. However, what value are these vitamins when rancid fat inhibits their absorption by the body?

Health authorities recommend 25 to 50 grams of fat in the daily diet of the average adult, but not more than 100 grams. The amount of fat should not be more than twenty percent of the total calories daily. In the diet of the healthiest groups of people in the tropical and temperate regions of the earth, fat is less than 10 percent of the total calorie intake. Those groups have far less heart disease.

It would seem reasonable to eat more unsaturated fats than saturated fats. Vegetable fats as a rule have a higher content of unsaturated fatty acids, which means that fats from vegetable sources are more beneficial than those from animal sources. At the same time, to keep these fats unsaturated, an adequate daily intake of vitamin C and vitamin E with meals, either from natural sources (preferably) or as a dietary supplement, is highly recommended.

Mercury and Metabolism

Here I would like to point out a fact that you may already be aware of, that Mercury and the sign that it rules, Virgo, play an intermediate role in body metabolism between the Mars-Saturn functions of catabolism (breakdown of complex molecules into simpler molecules) and the Venus-Jupiter functions of anabolism (construction of more complex molecules from simpler ones).

For example, in the small intestine, which is ruled by Virgo, the Mars-Saturn process of digestion comes to its logical conclusion. Then a discriminative process takes place with the products of digestion, which are rich in the raw materials that the body needs. The body takes in what it requires by selective absorption through the wall of the small intestine, passing on the residue to the large intestine for elimination. When the food is ready to be absorbed, the body receives a chemical signal.

The body receives two basic kinds of messages—tiny electrical impulses telegraphed over the nervous system and chemical messages carried by the bloodstream. Both types of messages are ruled by Mercury, messenger of the gods, and both types involve some discriminative function, which is the province of Virgo.

All along the metabolic trail, the body receives messages that turn on or turn off some vital process. Even when you sit down to eat or smell something cooking, the rich aromas and sights turn on the process of salivation in your mouth, signaling the body to be ready for digestion. The stomach cells begin to produce enzymes and hydrochloric acid. As the food is chewed, Mercury tells us to swallow. Mercury also tells the stomach when to release the partially digested food into the small intestine for final digestion and absorption.

One very important group of the body's chemical messengers is the hormones, which are discussed in more detail in Chapter Eight. While each hormone has its own planetary ruler, hormones as a class are ruled by Mercury. If Mercury in the horoscope is afflicted by squares and oppositions (and some conjunctions), Mercury sometimes sends out the wrong signals or signals at the wrong times. Things happen when they should not happen. Depending upon the planets involved and the severity of affliction, the results may range from loss of appetite or indigestion to multiple sclerosis, palsy or mental psychosis. Little Mercury thus symbolically plays a major role in making the various parts of the body work in unison to maintain good health, and it also plays a major role in disease. We can thus see that the mind is indeed very important in controlling the physical symptoms of disease.

Some Mercury functions are instinctive, or known from birth; others must be learned, which is where Gemini (learning), Mercury's other sign, comes in. At an early age you learned that ice cream tastes good. Think how good an ice cream sundae would taste right now, and notice that immediately your mouth begins to salivate. This is a *learned* response to an outside stimulus. On the other hand, you would not eat sawdust, because you have learned first hand or been told that sawdust does not taste good and has no food value. As we examine other body processes in the next chapter, we shall again point out Mercury's important role in turning on and off vital functions. Understanding Mercury's bodily symbolism thus leads us to a greater appreciation of all that this planet symbolizes in general astrology.

In this chapter I have explained what fat really is and its important role in keeping the body healthy. We have examined two important fatty substances—cholesterol and lecithin—and their role in metabolism. And finally we have looked at Mercury's role in controlling body processes generally.

In addition to learning more about some of the body's vital processes, I hope you are also gaining a finer appreciation and understanding of how the beautiful symbolism of astrology, developed long before mankind knew anything about biochemistry, chemistry or alchemy, fits into modern-day sophisticated concepts. What tremendous minds those ancient astrologer-priests had, to grasp the planetary correspondences so totally that only minor changes have had to be made in their basic planetary assignments!

I further hope that this new knowledge of what I like to call "astro-chemistry" will refine and deepen your understanding of traditional astrological concepts, which are rooted in the biochemistry of the body.

Now that we have examined the first steps in metabolism and have looked at the basic foods that the body requires, we are ready to find out what happens to this raw material once it has been absorbed in the intestines. To do this, we need to learn about the role played by enzymes (Chapter Seven) and by hormones (Chapter Eight).

7

ENZYMES:
BODY CATALYSTS

In this chapter we will find out what happens to the raw products of the digestive process after they are absorbed into the bloodstream through tiny blood vessels called capillaries in the walls of the small intestine. In order to clearly understand this process, we must first learn about the class of body compounds that are called enzymes.

What is an Enzyme?

The body can be thought of as a massive chemical plant in which thousands of different reactions take place simultaneously every minute of our lives. These chemical reactions are interdependent; if one fails to proceed properly, many other reactions are affected, which can result in sickness or disease. Good health thus means that all the reactions must take place at the right time, in the right place and in the proper proportion.

Every chemist knows that when certain proportions of particular chemicals are combined in the right circumstances, a predictable reaction will take place. A common example of this is the mixing of baking soda and lemon juice to produce carbon dioxide gas. This reaction occurs spontaneously when the reacting substances are mixed. However, most chemical reactions require some form of energy, usually heat. In other words, you have to heat up the substances to make them react. Most of the reactions that take place in the body require heat.

One type of chemical reaction, called oxidation, releases energy in the form of heat and sometimes light. This occurs whenever a substance combines with oxygen. Your car engine heats up because when gasoline is combined with the oxygen in the air and oxidized in the cylinders of the engine, considerable heat is released. A sudden oxidation reaction is called an explosion. Rapid oxidation is called a fire, which produces both heat and light. When oxidation occurs slowly, as in the tarnishing of a penny, only heat is released.

The body obtains all of its heat energy through oxidation. In each living plant or animal cell, oxygen from the air is combined with a simple sugar, usually glucose, to produce water, carbon dioxide and energy:

oxygen + sugar = carbon dioxide + water + energy

The water and carbon dioxide are of little use to the body and must be removed before they build up. It is *energy* that the body requires to fuel all of the other chemical reactions that take place in each cell. This very basic vital process was mentioned in Chapter Two under the symbolic astrological rulership of Leo–Aquarius, whose physiological keyword, you will remember, is "energizing."

In order for any chemical reaction to take place, the substances must be brought into intimate contact with each other. As long as the lemon juice remains in the bottle and the baking soda in its box, they cannot react. So it is within the body. The necessary raw ingredients are brought to the cells by the bloodstream, and they pass through the cell wall by a process called osmosis, as well as by other forms of selective absorption. They float around in solution in the cytoplasm, the liquid interior of the cell, along with the raw materials for many different reactions. The problem then is to bring the right materials together so that the reaction can occur.

This last step is carried out by the enzymes, which are electrically charged, proteinlike "collector molecules." Each kind of enzyme attracts the proper raw materials for a particular reaction, bringing them together so that they can react. The enzymes themselves do not enter into the reaction and can thus be thought of as catalysts. They can be called the cell's matchmakers; they arrange the marriage without entering into the relationship themselves. Since they are proteins, the enzymes eventually wear out and must be replaced.

There is a specific enzyme for almost every chemical reaction that occurs in the body, and each enzyme has only one function—to see that its particular reaction takes place. If the enzyme wears out and is not replaced, that reaction does not take place, and its vital products are not available as raw materials for the next reaction. Like a row of dominoes, each reaction depends on the previous one, and if one does not take place, a whole series of vital chemical reactions comes to a halt. Enzymes are extremely sensitive to temperature changes. They are at their efficient best at 98.6° F., and when the body is chilled or in fever, their ability to combine the raw materials is lessened.

Enzymes as a class are under the rulership of Pluto, as are all replicative processes, such as printing, xerography, cell reproduction and mass production techniques. Most chemical poisons, ruled by Neptune, are substances that actually combine with and destroy the enzymes. Observe the antagonistic Neptune–Pluto effect!

Enzymes are formed from ribonucleic acid (RNA) molecules in the cell. The RNA molecules, which are formed from the hereditary material (genes) in the cell nucleus, act as a template upon which the enzymes are formed. Pluto rules all of these processes. When a living organism is born with a defective gene or if a gene is missing, the RNA molecule is not complete, and thus some specific enzyme is not formed in the cell. The reaction that depends on this enzyme thus cannot occur, and the organism is defective. If the reaction is vital to the life of the organism, the organism will die without it.

Modern medicine recognizes a number of such hereditary defects caused by the absence of particular enzymes. Babies born with phenylketonuria (PKU), for example, are unable to use the amino acid called phenylalanine, which then builds up in the body and eventually poisons it. (Newborn babies are now routinely given a PKU test, so that treatment can begin immediately if this defect is present.) Modern astrology recognizes such genetic defects as planetary afflictions to Pluto.

Certain hereditary defects, or mutations, are not serious enough to cause death, but they do change the body chemistry. When such a change is passed on to the offspring, the evolution of the species is affected. For example, insects like the termite have enzymes that convert wood and other forms of cellulose into sugar. In the process of evolution, which often involves nonlethal mutations, the higher animals have lost this ability. Again, most animals other than man have an intestinal enzyme that allows manufacture of vitamin C when this vitamin is not part of the diet. As human beings evolved, this ability was lost, and thus it is vital to include vitamin C in the diet each day.

When bacteria and viruses attack the body, they interfere with normal enzyme functions, again resulting in a disease condition. Since bacteria and viruses are also ruled by Pluto, the Pluto functions of the body are subtly altered by their presence. Viruses are particularly subtle and insidious, for they are constructed of material very similar to the hereditary material in the cell's nucleus. Certain viruses can hook on to the nuclear template and cause the cell to manufacture a different type of RNA, thus producing new enzymes to satisfy the virus's needs. When the cell divides, the daughter cells are different from the parent cell, and we have what is commonly known as cancer. Medicine treats cancer (Pluto ruled) with drugs, ruled by Neptune. Again, notice the Pluto–Neptune antagonism.

Bacterial subversion of the normal cell chemistry is subtle, undercover, hidden and a form of sabotage—all of which are astrologically assigned to Pluto. It takes Neptune, Pluto's antithesis, to recognize this deception. This is why the physiological function of Pisces, ruled by Neptune, is to recognize foreign substances that enter the body and destroy or neutralize them, using antigen-antibody responses and the white blood cells. The thymus gland (Neptune ruled) plays a particularly important role in protecting the body from bacteria and viruses in early childhood while the body is learning to defend itself against attack by Pluto-ruled substances.

Earlier we discussed the two basic kinds of reactions that occur in the body—reactions in which complex chemical compounds are reduced to simpler ones and those in which simple compounds are combined to make more complex ones. If enzymes cause these reactions to occur, then the enzymes themselves must be ruled by the same planets that rule the reactions. The enzymes of analysis (catabolism), ruled by Saturn, break down the complex compounds into simpler ones, and the enzymes of synthesis (anabolism), ruled by Jupiter, reconstruct simple molecules into more complex ones. Pluto remains the general ruler of all enzymes; Jupiter and Saturn are the subrulers, according to the enzyme's function.

An example of a catabolic enzyme (ruled by Saturn) is rennin, found in the digestive juices of infants and children under two. Its function is to reduce the complex protein lactoglobulin, which is found in milk, into simpler substances. Another example is ptyalin, found in the saliva, whose function is to break down complex starch molecules into simpler sugar molecules. One of the anabolic enzymes (ruled by Jupiter) is the chlorophyll in plant cells, which combines water, carbon dioxide and the Sun's energy to form plant starch.

Unfortunately, chemists have not followed a uniform system for naming the various enzymes. However, any substance whose name ends in "ase" is an enzyme.

Composition of Enzymes

Each enzyme has a unique chemical formula. Most of the molecule is composed of protein, a string of amino acid units in a particular sequence that is characteristic of that kind of enzyme. But there is more to the enzyme molecule. Perhaps you have wondered why vitamins and minerals are so essential. The reason is that every enzyme molecule contains one kind of vitamin and one kind of mineral. The mineral gives the enzyme its electrical charge, which attracts oppositely charged raw materials that are required for the reaction it catalyzes. The vitamin completes the structure of the particular enzyme. The composition of the enzyme molecule is:

enzyme = protein + vitamin + mineral

The reason we need vitamins and minerals every day in our diet is to replace the enzymes that are continually wearing out. Chapter Ten of this book discusses the cell salts, which are nothing more than the minerals, in highly purified form, that the body needs to replace its worn-out enzymes. Healing arts practitioners who prescribe cell salts believe that many diseases are caused by the body's temporary inability to replace necessary enzymes. They feel that by supplying the raw materials in pure form, the body can more easily overcome the disease.

To see how enzymes work, let's take as an example the liver enzyme ethylase, which contains vitamin B-1, thiamine. Its function is to convert grain alcohol into carbon dioxide and water. If a person drinks too much alcohol, the ethylase cannot convert it all to carbon dioxide and water, so the person develops a hangover caused by the destruction of protein. All hangover remedies contain vitamin B-1 to help the liver replace the ethylase that is used up in the process of detoxifying the alcohol. Without this enzyme in the liver, alcohol would poison and destroy the body.

As an enzyme, ethylase is ruled by Pluto, and it is co-ruled by Saturn because it reduces the complex alcohol molecule into simpler substances. Alcohol, ruled by Neptune, can eventually be converted by the body to fat, which is ruled by Jupiter. Pluto vs. Neptune; Saturn vs. Jupiter! What a beautiful astrological picture of a physiological process!

Antagonistic Planetary Pairs

In the preceding chapters we have seen many examples of the astrological law of polarities as applied to the planets. These pairs are:

Sun vs. Moon
Venus vs. Mars
Jupiter vs. Saturn
Neptune vs. Pluto

When there is a health problem related to one of the planets in the four pairs mentioned above, we use as an antidote a substance ruled by the opposite planet, for example, drugs (Neptune) to treat bacterial invasion (Pluto).

What do we do with Mercury and Uranus? In my opinion, there is no substantial evidence to justify calling them antagonists. In fact they have much in common. Both have much to do with the mind, Mercury representing conscious thought and reason, Uranus representing intuition. And I do not feel that intuition is the antithesis of reason, for the only place where we are totally free is within our own mind, subject only to self-imposed limitations on the thinking process.

Mercury and Uranus can be called free-floaters, symbolizing alternative remedies to health problems. Since both represent the mind, these planets show us, as many practitioners of the healing arts are beginning to believe, that a person's mental attitude has a great deal to do with the prognosis of any disease condition. You do not have to apply the antagonistic planetary remedy if instead you apply Mercury, Uranus or both to help resolve the health problem.

The Liver

There is little doubt that the liver is the most important organ in controlling the body chemistry. Literally hundreds of enzyme-controlled reactions either take place within the liver or start here. That is why hepatitis (inflammation of the liver) and cirrhosis (deterioration of the liver) are such dangerous diseases. The liver not only purifies and detoxifies the blood, it also guards the entry of chemicals into the bloodstream. Before entering the general circulation, all food substances that are absorbed into the bloodstream in the stomach and the small intestine must pass through the liver via the portal circulation.

A major function of the liver, in addition to promoting growth, is to convert toxic substances that have been absorbed in the small intestine into harmless substances that can easily be eliminated in the urine. Many foods that we eat contain small quantities of potentially harmful substances. A good example is the benzoic acid in cranberries, which is toxic. However, an enzyme in the liver immediately converts the benzoic acid into hippuric acid, a harmless substance that is easily eliminated in the urine.

The liver does not have an enzyme to convert every potential poison. Ingesting even a small quantity of wood alcohol (methyl alcohol) results in blindness and often death, because the liver has no enzyme to protect the body from this poison.

The liver, which is undoubtedly ruled by Jupiter, is divided into several sections, called lobes. The upper lobes are generally assigned to Cancer, in which Jupiter is exalted. The lower lobes are assigned to Virgo, in which Jupiter is in its detriment. The reason for this dual sign rulership is that the liver is located in both the Cancer and Virgo areas of the body. Let's see what information we can derive from these sign and planet rulerships.

Jupiter rules growth processes and synthetic chemical reactions, and one function of the liver is to sustain and encourage growth. Jupiter also rules excesses, which is precisely what the liver seeks to keep under control. Physiologically, the lower lobes of the liver are primarily responsible for preventing large amounts of harmful substances from entering the general circulation, where they can harm the body. Astrologically, Virgo seeks to discriminate (the liver's function) and thus curtail the excesses represented by Jupiter. Persons with Jupiter in Virgo are not inclined to excesses.

Jupiter is in its exaltation in Cancer, ruled by the Moon, which controls the body's fluids. The liver deals with poisons by converting them to harmless substances that are eliminated by dilution with fluids (the Moon). Venus rules the kidneys, located in the Libra region of the body. Notice that the liver must interact harmoniously with the kidneys to eliminate the toxins. Venus is, of course, exalted in Pisces, which is co-ruled by Jupiter.

As noted earlier, Mercury has the quality of turning off either a Jupiter-Venus or a Saturn-Mars process in the body. Mercury rules Virgo, Jupiter's detriment. The Virgo rulership of the liver thus symbolizes how excessive eating and drinking are controlled by the liver's discriminative processes and also how large excesses, especially of drinking, can actually destroy the liver. Sensible, rational control (Mercury-Gemini-third house) or self-discipline (Saturn) is the antidote to excessive alcohol consumption. Dilution of alcohol by water (Jupiter and Neptune exalted in Cancer, the Moon's sign, which rules water) is another alternative. Here is additional evidence of how the dignities of the planets contribute to a greater understanding of the chemistry of the body.

Liver Disease and the Horoscope

Now that we understand the liver and its planetary and sign rulerships, we can find out how liver problems are shown symbolically in the horoscope. Although we use the liver as a specific example, the general principles outlined here apply to all disease conditions.

Certain diseases are hereditary, existing from the moment of conception because of a hereditary defect, such as lack of a particular enzyme. Such a defect would show up in the natal chart, generally in one of two ways, the most obvious being a Pluto affliction (heredity) to Jupiter (the liver). Recent research with midpoints also reveals a second sign. When a natal planet is located at the midpoint of Mars and Saturn (using very tight orbs of ± 1°), the vital processes or organs represented by that planet are likely to malfunction in some way. The most obvious manifestation is that the organ is underdeveloped or fails to function properly. Another critical midpoint is that of Saturn–Neptune. Neptune is in its detriment in Virgo, which rules discriminative processes, and Saturn is in its detriment in Aries, which rules regulative processes. The organ represented by the planet at the Saturn–Neptune midpoint either fails to respond to regulation or loses its power to discriminate or both. This manifests in the personality of the individual and/or in the functioning of the body.

The onset of a disease that is not hereditary, that develops at some specific time in a person's life, may be signaled by either a progressed or a transiting aspect to the natal planet that symbolizes the site of the disease. Or it may be signaled by a transiting or progressed planet at the midpoint of Mars–Saturn or Saturn–Neptune. Any astrology student interested in health and nutrition ought to note very carefully their two Mars–Saturn midpoints and their two Saturn–Neptune midpoints. (Every planetary pair has two midpoints). Transits or progressions to these points within an orb of ± 1° are often, but not always, symbolic of potential disease problems.

Let's see how these general rules apply to the liver. Jupiter afflicted by Pluto natally may indicate a genetic defect in the liver, such that it does not function properly. Jupiter afflicted by Saturn might mean that the liver doesn't respond to toxic substances as quickly as it should. One manifestation of this might be a very low tolerance for alcohol, a tendency to intoxication by very small amounts of alcohol. Also, Jupiter afflicted by Saturn (crystallizing diseases) often indicates gallstones. Jupiter afflicted by Neptune may indicate that the liver fails to identify toxic substances.

A progressed or transiting square, opposition or quincunx of Mars, representing inflammation, to Jupiter might signal the onset of hepatitis. A progressed or transiting square, opposition or quincunx of Saturn to Jupiter may result in the liver retaining excessive amounts of fat, which is also Jupiter ruled. Squares and oppositions are readily recognized by most astrologers as aspects of affliction, but not until recently did astrologers recognize the quincunx, or inconjunct, aspect of 150° as a major and often afflicting aspect.

A transit or progression of Jupiter to the Mars–Saturn midpoint may signal a rather sudden cessation of some important Jupiter function. A transit of Jupiter to the Saturn–Neptune midpoint may signal a temporary inability to either regulate and/or discriminate properly. As the transit or progression passes, the condition usually disappears, as long as permanent damage has not been done to the body.

We all have observed that diseases and afflictions have different effects on different individuals. Take the flu or common cold as an example. Some people are really knocked out when they contract the flu. Others recover quite quickly. Some persons who get hepatitis have to remain in bed for months; others recover in a couple of weeks. Why is this so? There are several reasons. First and foremost is the body's recuperative ability, its supply of life force as symbolized by the Sun. Those who have the Sun in an angular house, especially the first house, tend to recuperate very quickly. They have a larger amount of life force and resistance to disease. Those whose Sun is in a cadent house, especially the sixth or the twelfth, require a longer period to recuperate because their supply of life force or resistance is not so great.

A second factor is the sign location of the planet that represents the afflicted area or organ. Those who have Jupiter in either Sagittarius, Pisces or Cancer (Jupiter's three best sign locations) are much more likely to recover quickly from Jupiter afflictions. On the other hand, people with Jupiter in Gemini, Virgo or Capricorn usually need a longer period to recover and are much more susceptible to Jupiter-type afflictions.

Finally, in considering susceptibility to diseases, we cannot overlook the house positions of the planets. Planets located in the sixth or the twelfth house of the natal chart often symbolize potential health problems. For example, a person with Jupiter afflicted in Capricorn in the sixth house would be far more likely to have liver problems than a person with Jupiter afflicted in Capricorn in some other house. Usually the sixth house suggests acute conditions, those that come on suddenly but also clear up quickly with proper treatment. The twelfth house deals more with chronic conditions, those that last a long time and are likely to require hospitalization.

The information in this chapter covers an area that is not usually addressed in other books on nutrition. For some reason, most of the popular books on nutrition say very little, if anything, about the enzymes. Yet enzymes are vital to the basic chemistry of the body, and an understanding of their function is vital to any sensible diet-planning program. I have tried to make clear that the function of enzymes is to catalyze the hundreds of chemical reactions that must take place continually in the body in order to maintain good health. I have pointed out how enzymes are classified, the conditions under which they work, how they are constructed and replaced as they wear out, and how the beautiful symbolism of astrology helps us understand them.

When you analyze your own natal chart, you will undoubtedly wish to refer to this chapter to refresh your mind about the basic techniques. First select the planet and sign that relate to the site of the health problem you are studying. Note where these factors are located in the wheel, how the planet is aspected, where the Sun is located by house and sign, and where the Mars–Saturn and Saturn–Neptune midpoints are. With this information, you have the basic tools to start your analysis.

8

HORMONES:
CHEMICAL MESSENGERS

In this chapter we discuss the regulative role in the metabolism played by the potent biochemical compounds called hormones. We will relate them to their source in the body and to their planet and sign rulerships, and we will see how certain planetary afflictions affect these regulative processes. The importance of the diet is also discussed.

The Role of Hormones

Scattered throughout the body are the endocrine glands, which secrete directly into the bloodstream very small amounts of hormones, which generally speed up or slow down some vital chemical process in the body. Hormones have a profound effect on both the physical body and on the personality, and thus they strongly influence our behavior. This is perhaps most evident at the onset of puberty, when the body increases its production of sex hormones. The hormones have a regulative effect, which puts them under the general rulership of Aries and Libra. In fact, many of the endocrine glands are actually located in the Aries and Libra sections of the body. Afflictions related to these signs can put the endocrine system out of balance. In addition, each of the endocrine glands and the hormone it produces is ruled by a particular planet.

However, hormones may also be thought of as chemical

messengers. Secreted in one area of the body, they signal a reaction in another area to speed up or slow down. This puts the hormones under the general rulership also of Mercury, the messenger.

The human body is bilaterally symmetrical; that is, many organs and structures occur in pairs, one on each side of the body. The right and left organs act as back-ups for each other. The Sun is the general ruler of all the organs on the right side of the body; the Moon is the general ruler of those on the left—with one very important exception. The Moon controls the right half of the brain; the Sun, the left half. Other than that, the right eye, ear, nostril, breast, arm, kidney, testicle, ovary and leg are under the general rulership of the Sun; the corresponding organs on the left are controlled by the Moon.

All of these co-rulerships may seem a bit confusing. Max Heindel, in his book *The Message of the Stars*, helps sort it out with a good analogy. Heindel says: "It is as when we say that all who live in the United States of America are citizens of that country, but some are subject to the laws of California, others to those of Maine." Aries–Libra, Mercury, the Sun and/or the Moon correspond in this analogy to the whole country, while planets that rule particular endocrine glands correspond to the states.

In general, an oversecretion of one of the endocrine glands is related to Jupiter; an undersecretion is indicated by Saturn; tumors of these glands are generally Pluto-related; and infection or inflammation is related to Mars. The connection is generally a square, opposition, quincunx or sometimes a conjunction between the ruler of the gland and the appropriate planet, with a sixth or twelfth house involvement.

The Pituitary Gland

The pituitary gland, which is ruled by Uranus and Scorpio, is called the master control gland of the body. Not only does it regulate growth and reproductive functions, it also regulates the other endocrine glands as well. It is a tiny red pea-shaped gland located deep within the brain for protection. It has two distinct lobes, each of which has a special function. The anterior, or front, lobe rules the reproductive forces and the nerve fibers. The hormones it secretes trigger ovulation in the female and the onset of puberty in both sexes. Afflictions to Uranus, especially from Aries, can cause such medical conditions as precocious puberty (the premature development of secondary sex characteristics—as early as age five or six) and overstimulation of the other endocrine glands, producing all sorts of physical malfunctions.

The posterior lobe of the pituitary gland controls circulation of fluids within the body, especially to the kidneys. Over- or undersecretion of the hormones in this lobe can cause a person to develop as a midget or as a giant. The natal charts of such freaks of nature usually show Uranus as the causative agent, acting too freely on the pituitary gland. This gland is vital to the control of nutrition and assimilation of food and is often implicated in diseases like arthritis. Uranus is in its fall position in Taurus, which sometimes indicates diminished activity of the posterior lobe of the pituitary, principally through the pituitary's close relationship to the thyroid gland, which is located in the Taurus region of the body.

Occultists consider the pituitary very important in understanding our spiritual nature, for it is thought to be a spiritual center of our being. And it is said to be stimulated or awakened by trine or sextile transits of Neptune or Uranus to the natal position of Uranus. In any case, medical authorities are now reasonably certain that the posterior pituitary regulates the nutrition and growth of the body. Jupiter represents the principle of growth, which is frequently shown in natal charts through Jupiter aspects of Uranus. The South Node of the Moon, when close to the Ascendant, may retard physical growth, according to a study reported by George White in his book, *The Moon's Nodes and Their Importance in Natal Astrology.*

The Thyroid Gland

Closely linked to the pituitary is the thyroid gland, the master regulator of the rate of metabolism. Located in the throat area, the thyroid is ruled by Mercury and Taurus. Its hormone, thyroxin, is secreted directly into the bloodstream. The thyroid gland's role in maintaining good health can hardly be overestimated, since thyroxin regulates the body temperature, controls growth rate and regulates the rate at which food is oxidized. To a very great extent, this gland influences our mental and emotional balance.

The hormone thyroxin is composed of the amino acid tyrosine, which comes from the protein we eat, and the mineral iodine, which must be present in the daily diet. As we shall discuss later, iodine is ruled by the Sun, and people who have the Sun in Taurus or Scorpio frequently require more iodine in their diet for normal thyroid function.

Thyroid disorders fall into two general classes: 1) lack of sufficient iodine in the diet to produce the required amount of thyroxin, and 2) a body disorder that creates such a demand for thyroxin that the thyroid gland cannot fulfill it. Astrologically, the first condition is often symbolized by a malefic aspect of Saturn to the Sun (which rules iodine), while the latter condition is generally a malefic aspect of Jupiter to the planet that rules the body region demanding the excessive amount of thyroxin. In the first case, the thyroid gland usually enlarges to try to produce the necessary amount of thyroxin (and iodine), and we see what is commonly called goiter. A classic astrological indicator of goiter is an afflicted Venus in Taurus with a sixth-house involvement.

Atrophy of the thyroid gland produces cretinism in children and myxoedema when it occurs later in life. Intelligence is impaired, idiocy is not uncommon and physical development is severely impaired. The astrological signature of this condition is generally a severe affliction to Mercury, generally from Saturn. On the other hand, an oversupply of thyroxin causes hyperthyroidism, with excessive nervousness, hyperactivity and protruding eyeballs. Usually this condition is indicated by a Mars or Jupiter affliction to Mercury, especially the square.

Iodine is best supplied to the diet through foods from the ocean—fish, shellfish and ocean plants like kelp. It is also found in sea salt, which is of great benefit to those who live far from the ocean. Drinking water contaminated with cyanides can also contribute to goiter, as can excessive amounts of barbiturates, when there is insufficient iodine or vitamin C (ruled by Saturn) in the diet. The foods that contain trace amounts of natural cyanide, such as cabbage and almonds, also contain large amounts of vitamin C to counterbalance the cyanide. But this helps only when we do not cook all of the water-soluble vitamin C out of the food.

The Islets of Langerhans

The pancreas, once thought to be an endocrine gland, has subsequently been found to have two major functions, one for digestion and one for hormonal control of carbohydrate metabolism. The pancreas produces a fluid that is rich in enzymes that are essential to final digestion of fats, proteins and carbohydrates. Pancreatic fluid is released into the small intestine, not the bloodstream. However, within the pancreas is a series of tiny glands, not related to the pancreas, called the islets of Langerhans, named for the man who discovered them. These glands secrete directly into the bloodstream the hormone insulin, which plays a vital role in carbohydrate metabolism. Insulin controls the sugar level in the bloodstream and the rate at which the body stores sugar temporarily as animal starch or glycogen. Its effect is like the wick of a candle, in that the wax (sugar) will not burn without a wick (insulin). Undersecretion or total lack of insulin produces the metabolic disease called diabetes. Oversecretion of insulin causes the condition called low blood sugar or hypoglycemia. In this latter disease, the islets of Langerhans have been oversensitized and thus stimulated to produce excessive insulin. Because the blood sugar level remains low, the hypoglycemic person is continually hungry and tired.

The islets of Langerhans, glycogen, insulin and fat are all ruled by Jupiter. Sugar (glucose) is ruled by Venus. Because fat retards insulin production, it must be practically eliminated from the diet of diabetics and added to the diet of hypoglycemics. In the natal chart, Jupiter is at the heart of both disease conditions. With diabetics, Jupiter is restricted in its expression, typically by some Saturn affliction, while with hypoglycemia, Jupiter is afflicted (sensitized) by Neptune. In diabetes it is also quite common to find Jupiter in Aries, Libra or Scorpio natally and in the first, sixth or twelfth house, or the afflicting planet in one of these houses, particularly the sixth. If this pattern is not found in the natal chart, it often occurs in the progressed chart at the onset of diabetes in later life. Recent medical research has established a definite link between diabetes in later life and mumps in youth. The mumps virus apparently sensitizes the islets of Langerhans in some manner that is not yet completely understood. A rather high percentage of older diabetics had mumps in their youth, and it is strongly recommended that those who have had mumps in their youth have their blood sugar level carefully checked in an annual checkup.

The Adrenal Glands

The adrenal glands are two pea-shaped glands located above each kidney. Located in the Libra zone of the body, they are ruled by Mars. Anatomically they are divided into two distinct regions, the outer cortex and the inner medulla. Each region performs its own function and secretes its own particular hormones into the blood. The adrenal cortex secretes the hormone cortin, and the medulla, adrenalin. Both hormones are required for sugar metabolism. Cortin turns glycogen slowly back into glucose to maintain the proper blood sugar level between meals. Its effect is the opposite of insulin. Adrenalin has the same effect as cortin, except that it is much more immediate, almost instantaneous. It is released when the body is threatened and prepares it for "fight or flight."

The adrenal cortex also produces sex hormones called ketosteroids and adrenocorticosteroids, which the body manufactures from cholesterol. Perhaps the best known of the corticosteroids is cortisone, which is vital in the body's resistance to disease. Cortisone's planetary ruler has not yet been firmly established, but it is probably Mars. The adrenal cortex and the anterior portion of the pituitary gland are closely linked. The anterior pituitary produces a substance called ACTH (adreno-cortico-tropic hormone), which stimulates the production of corticosteroids by the adrenal cortex.

Either underactivity or overactivity of the adrenal glands can have serious health consequences, especially in a person's resistance to disease. In both men and women, the adrenal glands produce female sex hormones. In the male, the adrenal sex hormones are balanced by the male sex hormones produced by the testes. Insufficient adrenocortical hormone production has recently been linked to alcoholism. A person's tolerance for alcohol is directly linked to the amount of this hormone produced by the body. Overindulgence in alcohol damages the adrenal cortex, resulting in diminished hormone production and then addiction. Individuals with adrenocortical insufficiency show decreased metabolism, low blood pressure, a characteristic hair distribution and a craving for salt or sweets.

The characteristic astrological pattern for adrenal hormone insufficiency is an affliction to Mars from Jupiter, Saturn or, most frequently, Neptune or a combination of these. A Neptune–Mars square, opposition or inconjunct is often found in the natal charts of alcoholics as well as in the charts of teetotalers who recognize that they can't tolerate alcohol.

The Testes and Ovaries

The ovaries and testes, in addition to producing ova and sperm, also produce sex hormones, which are released into the bloodstream. The testes produce the two major male sex hormones, testosterone and androsterone. The ovaries produce estrogen and progesterone, female sex hormones that control the menstrual cycle to a large extent. Both organs are in the Scorpio region of the body and are ruled by Mars. The actual act of conception, the fusion of sperm and egg, with its hereditary results, is ruled by Pluto, the "alpha and omega" of the planets.

Again, malfunction of these glands is generally indicated by Mars afflicted by Saturn, Neptune or occasionally Uranus, with Mars or the afflicting planets located in Scorpio or Aries natally, by progression or by transit.

The Thymus Gland

Until recently, the thymus gland, which is located in the upper thorax near the throat, was badly misunderstood and underrated by the medical profession. This gland is largest during puberty, after which it begins to shrink, so it was thought to be unimportant during adulthood. Earlier medical astrologers assigned this gland to Venus, which was a serious mistake. The thymus gland is actually ruled by Neptune, which explains in part why it took so long for medicine to ascertain its true function, for Neptune obscures all it comes in contact with.

Pisces, ruled by Neptune, rules the lymphatic system as well as the feet. It is in the lymphatic system rather than the circulatory system where the white blood cells fight off viral or bacterial infection, as evidenced by the swollen lymph nodes in the neck, underarm, scalp or groin when such battles are taking place. The thymus gland secretes a hormone called thymosin, whose basic function is to alert the body's defense mechanism to attack by foreign organisms. Children who have underactive thymus glands are particularly susceptible to bacterial and viral infections, to the point that some must receive injections of thymosin (also Neptune ruled), which is produced from beef thymus glands. The thymus requires lots of vitamin A.

Little is known about hyperactivity of the thymus gland, but underactivity is generally related to a malefic aspect to Neptune from Saturn, often with one of these planets in Taurus (the neck region).

The Pineal Gland

Of all the ductless or endocrine glands, the pineal gland, a small, reddish body in the posterior portion of the skull cavity, is causing the greatest disagreement among astrologers as to its function and significance. Cornell describes it as "the third eye—the spiritual center of the body—the organ of spiritual sight and spirituality—the seat of the soul in the body—the organ of thought transference," and many people feel that this gland is related in some way to extrasensory perceptive powers. Its ruler is probably Neptune, or possibly Uranus.

We know that for a short period after a baby is born, the top of its skull is not completely ossified, or enclosed by bone. Until recently it was presumed that the only reason for this was to give the skull flexibility during the birth process and to prevent brain damage. While this is probably true, recent research has revealed that during the first days after birth a certain amount of diffuse light penetrates the skull through the fontanel and triggers a whole series of enzyme reactions as light strikes the pineal body. Apparently these enzymatic reactions are essential in starting the baby's metabolic processes.

A new school of astrological thought in England holds that the more light this region is exposed to before the skull closes, the more psychically sensitive the child will become. Also they believe that astrologers are wrong in using as the birth moment the time when the child takes its first breath; rather they perceive the true birth moment as the time when the top of the skull emerges into the light. This is an interesting theory, which is supportable biochemically. The temporary opening in the skull, the fontanel, has been much written about in occult literature. Science still has much to learn about the pineal body, ruled by Neptune, for its function is quite obscure.

The Spleen

Most astrological discussions of the endocrine glands include the spleen, located in the Virgo region of the body, even though it doesn't seem to produce any specific hormones. Its planetary ruler is generally conceded to be the Sun, and any afflictions to the spleen are generally related to Saturn. The spleen and bone marrow are the sources of white corpuscles, which are so necessary in fighting invasions of bacteria and virus. As we pointed out earlier, this fight occurs in the lymphatic system, ruled by Pisces—Virgo's opposite sign.

Esoteric astrology places great emphasis on the spleen, claiming that the solar forces enter the body through this organ. The spleen is said to be the focal point of the astral body and the connecting point between the physical and astral worlds. The lower dorsal vertebrae, the area of the spine that houses and protects the nerves to the spleen, is also said to be important, in that any blockage here to the splenic nerves impedes the vital energies entering the body.

To the medical doctor and the physiologist, the spleen is vital to the normal protective mechanisms of the body. As aging occurs and the bone marrow is used up, the spleen becomes even more important as the source of blood cells. It is involved in many forms of anemia as well as leukemia, and injury to or removal of the spleen affects the body's defense against disease.

The Parathyroid Glands

No discussion of hormones or the endocrine glands would be complete without some discussion of the two pairs of parathyroid glands, located in the neck close to the thyroid gland. They play an especially vital role in the metabolism of calcium. Their discovery is comparatively recent.

An insufficiency of parathyroid hormone in the blood results in a decrease of calcium in the blood, a condition known as tetany. Too much parathyroid hormone in the blood may be involved in excessive calcium being present in the system, which can result in calcification of several of the internal organs. Removal of the parathyroids can result in nervous irritability, tetany, convulsions and, ultimately, death. Hypoparathyroidism (undersecretion) results in a lowered blood calcium level and a higher than normal blood phosphate level. It is presently believed that parathyroid hormone increases urinary secretion of phosphate, which increases the blood concentration of calcium.

Saturn, which rules calcium, is thought to be the ruler of the parathyroid glands, but Pluto is also thought to influence them strongly, because Mars and Pluto co-rule phosphate.

We have seen in this chapter the vital role that hormones play in good nutrition and health. The body forms these hormones from the foods we eat, many from unsaturated fats and proteins. Mercury is the general ruler of all hormones, because hormones secreted in one part of the body act as chemical messengers to other areas.

Each hormone and the endocrine gland that secretes it is ruled by a particular planet and by the sign that controls that body region. In the older astrological literature, the rulerships of the various endocrine glands are quite confused, because at that time physiology was not well understood. For example, Heindel and others speak of the spinal fluid as an etheric substance, which we know is untrue; it is a liquid of high protein content. However, while their specific knowledge of physiology was somewhat lacking, the ancients were remarkably accurate in assigning many rulerships.

When Jupiter, Saturn, Pluto or Mars (or sometimes Neptune) is located in the sixth or the twelfth house and in malefic aspect to the planet that rules one of the endocrine glands, there may be overactivity, underactivity, tumors or inflammation of that gland. This seems to be true also when the afflicted ruler is located in the sixth or the twelfth house.

In many cases the disease condition can be corrected or alleviated by taking particular vitamins, minerals or cell salts that are associated with the afflicted planet and/or the sign on the cusp of the sixth and/or the twelfth house—usually a combnation of substances related to the signs on the sixth and the twelfth house cusps.

9

VITAMINS
IN THE DIET

In earlier chapters I have mentioned the importance of vitamins in nutrition. Very little was known about vitamins before 1900, and even now, more vitamins are being discovered. Our present knowledge of these substances, though considerable, should not be considered complete. One thing is certain, however: a considerable number of chemical substances, which we call by the generic name "vitamins," are absolutely essential in the daily diet for good health. Although we call them all vitamins, they have very little similarity to each other. Many animals are able to manufacture these substances as part of their metabolism: man, in the process of evolving, has lost this ability and must obtain vitamins through his food. For example, many animals, including dogs, can manufacture vitamin C from the food they eat. Humans cannot synthesize vitamin C, and thus we must eat foods that contain this vitamin.

I have tried to emphasize in previous chapters that although the human metabolism is generally uniform, there are some striking hereditary differences among individuals in the ability to assimilate the various substances that are essential to good health. As a correlary to this, people who metabolize certain substances with difficulty must increase the quantity of those substances in their diet in order to minimize potential deficiencies.

Each of the vitamins has been assigned a planetary ruler,

and these rulers are discussed in this chapter. As a general rule, the vitamins that a person metabolizes with difficulty, and thus requires more of in the diet, are those ruled by the planet that rules the sign opposite his or her Sun sign. For example, take someone whose Sun is in Scorpio. Taurus, ruled by Venus, is opposite Scorpio, and that person's diet should include increased amounts of the vitamins ruled by Venus. The absorption of Venus-ruled substances will be enhanced by ingesting at the same time Mars-ruled substances, since Mars co-rules Scorpio. Not only are the substances related to your Sun sign most easily digested, but they facilitate the absorption of the substances ruled by the planet ruling the Sun's opposite sign. Again, we see the importance of the sign polarities.

Before discussing the individual vitamins, I would like to explain that we can subclassify the vitamins into two groups—those that are water soluble and those that are oil soluble. The Moon is the general ruler of the water-soluble vitamins; Neptune rules those that are oil soluble. Because of your basic hereditary makeup, if your Sun is in Capricorn, you probably need increased amounts of all the water-soluble vitamins; if your Sun is in Virgo, you probably need increased amounts of all the oil-soluble vitamins.

Oil-Soluble Vitamins

VITAMIN A. The Sun is the planetary ruler of this vitamin, which is often called the anti-infective or anti-ophthalmic-disease vitamin. Those with their Sun in Aquarius need increased amounts of vitamin A, which according to recent research, helps to prevent the formation of cancerous cells. Pluto, ruler of cancerous growths, is exalted in Aries, as is the Sun.

Vitamin A improves night vision and is especially important in maintaining the lining cells of the body, especially the cells of the skin, eyes, bones, teeth and the gastro-intestinal and urinary tracts. It is essential in resisting the attack of disease organisms, especially viruses. Insufficient vitamin A has been linked to the inability to gain weight, to baldness and to various problems of the genito-urinary tract. Libra, which rules this area, is the fall position of the Sun. Lack of vitamin A also leads to infection of the middle ear, which is ruled and strongly influenced by Aquarius. The richest natural sources of this vitamin are colored fruits and vegetables, dairy products, eggs, margarine, fish and liver.

VITAMIN D. This is the second of the oil-soluble vitamins. It too is ruled by the Sun, and thus those born under Aquarius need increased amounts of this vitamin also. However, unlike vitamin A, vitamin D can be synthesized by the body from cholesterol in the presence of sunlight. That is why it is called the "sunshine vitamin." Vitamins A and D are the two vitamins that can be harmful in too-large amounts. Remember, too much of a good thing can be as bad as too little. Have you ever spent a day in the bright sun at the beach and left with a headache? This is caused by too much vitamin D. After it is synthesized by the skin, vitamin D is stored principally in the liver.

This vitamin, along with parathyroid hormone, regulates the absorption and fixation of both phosphorus and calcium in the blood and thus regulates bones and teeth, which is why it is especially important in the diet of growing children. Now vitamin D is commonly added to milk. Insufficient vitamin D causes rickets and soft bones and teeth. Those with the Sun in Aquarius or with Saturn in Leo need more vitamin D in their diet than the average person.

The richest natural sources of vitamin D are fish oils, eggs, salmon, tuna, sardines and fortified milk. Some exposure to the Sun each day also aids greatly, because cholesterol in the skin manufactures vitamin D in the presence of sunlight.

VITAMIN E. The third of the oil-soluble vitamins, also called tocopherol, is ruled by Venus. For some time there was great controversy as to its value in human nutrition, although it was known to be essential in the diet of laboratory animals for reproduction. While early claims that vitamin E restores sexual vigor in both sexes are probably somewhat exaggerated, its value is now undisputed by nutritionists. Human milk contains four times the amount of vitamin E found in cow's milk, which tells us something of its importance. It also has great power to build and support tissue and is often used in the treatment of emphysema and varicose veins to strengthen the walls of capillaries. In areas of high air pollution, extra vitamin E is essential to protect the tiny air sacs in the lungs.

Recent Canadian research has established many other important nutritional uses for this vitamin; American doctors have been much more conservative in accepting these claims. Bread and butter go well together nutritionally, because the vitamin E in bread helps digest the butter fat and convert it into energy. Wheat germ is particularly high in this vitamin, as are cereal grains, meat, eggs, margarine and leafy vegetables when not overcooked. Nuts and legumes, such as beans, lentils and peas, are also rich sources of vitamin E. People who have the Sun in Aries or Scorpio have a greater need for vitamin E.

VITAMIN F. This is the name given to the group of essential unsaturated fatty acids, such as linoleic acid, which we discussed in Chapter Six. They are essential in preventing build-up of cholesterol. The richest sources of vitamin F are vegetable and fish oils, some animal oils, butter, cream, egg yolk, nuts and avocado. Jupiter is probably the ruler of this vitamin.

DAILY REQUIREMENTS. As I have stressed, too much of a good thing can be as harmful as not enough, and this rule applies particularly to vitamins A and D. Excessive quantities of these two oil-soluble vitamins can damage the liver, where they are stored. A normal diet does not contain excessive amounts of these vitamins, but supplementary vitamins A and D in large quantities can be harmful. The normal amounts for good health should be about as follows:

vitamin A: 10,000 to 20,000 units daily
vitamin D: 2,500 to 5,000 international units daily

vitamin E: 800 units in the form of d-alpha-
             tocopherol seems reasonable, al-
             though this amount has not yet been
             established.
Foods containing oil-soluble vitamins should not be
cooked too long in oil, because fats absorb and remove them.

Water-Soluble Vitamins

VITAMIN C. This extremely important vitamin, also
called ascorbic acid, is ruled by Saturn. It is essential in protein
metabolism (Saturn-ruled) and is important in the formation of
collagen, which gives cells their shape; note Capricorn's structural function here. Damage to the skin, which is ruled by
Saturn, is one of the first signs of vitamin C deficiency, a condition called scurvy. Many nutritional authorities believe that a
large number of Americans have borderline cases of scurvy
because of insufficient vitamin C on a daily basis.

As mentioned previously, vitamin C is an antioxidant,
which prevents unsaturated fats from oxidizing during digestion. Vitamin C is highly sensitive to heat, air or enzymes in
food, which cause it to oxidize and become a compound that is
useless to the body and may in fact be toxic. The normal
minimum requirement of vitamin C is about 30 to 100
milligrams per day, but smokers should take extra doses of this
vitamin. Every cigarette you smoke destroys 10 to 15 milligrams
of vitamin C, which is why heavy smoking accelerates the aging
process, ruled by Saturn.

Acerola and rose hips are rich natural sources of vitamin
C, as are the citrus fruits, especially grapefruit, and parsley, pep-
pers, guava, currants, kale, collards and tomatoes. While
vitamin C is known to be important in the body's resistance to
disease, there is at present considerable controversy as to
whether massive amounts of it are effective in preventing and
treating colds caused by viruses. Linus Pauling is the leading advocate of the benefits of massive doses, but other authorities

claim that this does not help much and may in fact be toxic. In this case astrology is not of much help in settling the controversy. Viruses, which are toxic, are ruled by Pluto. Since Pluto rules Scorpio, and Scorpio is not included among Saturn's dignities, we might conclude that vitamin C would be ineffective against viruses. It probably is. Saturn is exalted in Libra, which is Pluto's fall dignity. But I do not consider this evidence conclusive. The most effective vitamins against viruses ought to be vitamin E and niacin, since Pluto is in its fall in Libra and in its detriment in Taurus, both of which are ruled by Venus and thus antagonistic to Pluto.

VITAMIN P. This vitamin, which accompanies natural vitamin C as bioflavonoid, has no established planetary ruler as yet, but it is probably also ruled by Saturn, since deficiency results in bleeding and hemorrhage of the capillaries. Hemorrhage and bleeding are ruled by Mars, and Aries is ruled by Mars. And when Saturn is in Aries, it is in its fall. Cancer is also the detriment of Saturn, and insufficient vitamin P results in dropsy and seepage of water (Cancer rules body fluids) into the body cavities.

The minimum daily requirement of vitamin P has not been established, but those with the Sun in Cancer probably need more of both vitamin C and vitamin P. The citrus fruits are a good natural source of this vitamin.

VITAMIN K. The rulership of this vitamin, also called menadione, has not been clearly established, but I believe that it is probably Jupiter, since vitamin K is so important to proper liver function and is often administered in cases of liver disease, especially hepatitis. It is particularly important in the blood-clotting process and in the growth of newborn infants. One half milligram per day is considered sufficient to good health and normal clotting. It appears to play an important role in fat metabolism also.

Rich natural sources of vitamin K include alfalfa sprouts, soybean oil, egg yolk and leafy vegetables. Those who eliminate eggs from their diet for fear of cholesterol may be depriving themselves of the best source of vitamin K.

The B-Complex Vitamins

Vitamin B complex is the generic term for a rather large group of chemically unrelated compounds that share certain characteristics. All of the B vitamins are water soluble. In nature they usually occur as a group and are less effective when taken separately. All of them are important in the health of the liver and the nervous system, and all are used by the body in the synthesis of certain enzymes.

VITAMIN B-1. This vitamin, also called thiamine, is ruled by Mercury, and since Mercury also rules the nervous system, we have a clue to one of the major uses of thiamine, that is, maintaining the health of the nervous system. It is also used by the liver to manufacture enzymes that protect the body from toxic substances such as ethyl alcohol. Most of these poisons, including alcohol, are enemies of the central nervous system. In large quantities, thiamine also nourishes the skin and protects it by giving it an odor that we cannot detect but that biting insects dislike. Thiamine plays an especially important role in the metabolism of carbohydrates, and one symptom of vitamin B-1 deficiency is an increased craving for sweets. Without thiamine, sugar, ruled by Venus, cannot provide the body with energy. Note that Venus is in its fall in Virgo, Mercury's sign.

Deficiency of this vitamin is also shown in loss of appetite, insomnia, irritability, numbness in the extremities, poor digestion, weakness, slowed pulse, lowered blood pressure, constipation and sometimes an enlarged heart. The minimum daily requirement has been established as about 1 to 2 milligrams. Whole grain products, especially wheat germ, and yeast, milk, liver, eggs and many nuts are rich sources of this vitamin. Since it is water-soluble, thiamine is lost when food is cooked in water; it does not dissolve in oils or fats.

VITAMIN B-2. This vitamin, also called riboflavin or vitamin G, is ruled by the Moon. In combination with vitamin A (Sun-Moon combination!), it is especially important in carbohydrate metabolism, and it aids in the assimilation of protein and iron. While this vitamin is a rather stable chemical compound, it is affected or destroyed by light—remember its Moon rulership! It is thought to delay the aging process and to increase the body's defense against infection.

The Moon is in its detriment in Capricorn, which represents the skin and aging, and in its fall in Scorpio, which is co-ruled by Mars. Mars rules iron, so you would expect riboflavin to be important in the assimilation of iron. And since Scorpio rules reproduction and sexual power, you'd expect insufficient riboflavin to inhibit these normal processes as well. In fact, riboflavin is one of the best examples of the relation between astrological symbolism and nutrition. The Moon rules most eye-related diseases, and one of the first symptoms of riboflavin deficiency is impaired vision. Cataracts also result from riboflavin deficiency. While this is a Sun-related disease, the Sun and Moon are almost always conjunct or opposed, natally or by progression or transit, when a person has cataracts. And frequently in this condition, Saturn is the planet in oriental apearance (immediately preceding the Sun). Another sign of vitamin B-2 deficiency is stomach cramps, and the stomach is ruled by Cancer and the Moon. Still another sign is impaired hearing and ear infections; the right ear is ruled by Saturn and the left by Mars! Also, with riboflavin ruled by the Moon, it is not surprising that a deficiency makes a person's eyes especially sensitive to strong light.

The daily requirement of riboflavin is about 3 to 4 milligrams, which is approximately one and a half to two times the daily requirement of thiamine. Those with their Sun or Saturn in Capricorn or their Sun in Scorpio seem to require slightly more. Calf liver is probably the richest natural source of this vitamin, and other good sources are kidneys, milk, cheese, broccoli, the outer leaves of most green, leafy vegetables, which many people discard, and carrots, peanuts, apples and citrus fruits, as well as the sources of vitamin B-1.

VITAMIN B-6. With B-6, or pyridoxine, ruled by Jupiter, we have some excellent examples of astrological symbolism, especially concerning Jupiter's dignities. First, it is important to note that insufficient pyridoxine inhibits the assimilation of all the other B vitamins. And for vitamin B-6 to function properly, there must also be sufficient amounts of the mineral magnesium, ruled by the Sun (see Chapter Ten), in the diet. Whenever you take extra B-6, you ought to also take a small amount of dolomite, which is a good source of magnesium. Vitamin B-6 is especially important to good muscle function, insulin production by the pancreas and conversion of glucose to energy.

A look at the symptoms of B-6 deficiency provides some interesting astrological insights. First, Jupiter rules Sagittarius, and Sagittarius rules the muscles in the upper legs. Deficiency of B-6 produces muscular weakness and a characteristic shuffling gait. Jupiter is in its detriment in Gemini and Virgo, both of which are ruled by Mercury, which rules the nervous system. Lack of B-6 thus results in palsy, dizziness, nervousness and sometimes Parkinson's disease, which is characterized by trembling of the limbs. Since Virgo rules the area of the body containing the pancreas, and Jupiter rules the liver and the islets of Langerhans in the pancreas, which produce insulin, you'd expect insufficient B-6 to particularly affect these organs, and it does! With Jupiter in its fall in Capricorn, which rules the skin, insufficient B-6 causes swollen, red, cracked and sore skin. And finally, with Jupiter exalted in Cancer, which with the Moon rules the distribution of body fluids, it is not surprising to learn that B-6 helps distribute water in the tissues, especially in adipose or fatty tissue—remember, Jupiter rules fat! Lack of B-6 causes excessive fatty deposits of cholesterol in the circulatory system. Supplementary B-6 is used to relieve suffering from hemorrhoids and vaginitis (Scorpio-ruled Mars is exalted in Capricorn). What fabulous clues nutritional astrology provides!

Approximately 2 to 3 milligrams is the established daily requirement for vitamin B-6, but considerably more does not hurt, especially in the diet of people who are excessively nervous or under great stress for long periods of time. Stress causes the body to use B-6 more quickly. Those with their Sun or Mercury in Gemini or with Saturn in Virgo, Gemini or Capricorn should add extra B-6 to their diet along with a good source of magnesium. Rich natural sources of pyridoxine include liver and other organ meats, brewer's yeast, fish, wheat germ, egg yolk, cantaloupe, cabbage, milk and honey.

VITAMIN B-12. The ruler of B-12, or cobalamin, the "red vitamin," is of course Mars, which rules the color red. Mars also rules iron, and B-12 is intimately related to the assimilation of iron and the formation of red blood cells. Also, insufficient B-12 results in anemia because of insufficient iron in the system. This vitamin is in fact used in the treatment of anemia. B-12 contains the metal cobalt, also ruled by Mars. The body is capable of synthesizing some B-12, but only if there are traces of zinc, ruled by Uranus, exalted in Scorpio, Mars' sign.

Besides causing anemia, insufficient B-12 prevents production of the sex hormones (Mars and Scorpio ruled) and causes underdevelopment or shriveling of the breasts and sex organs. Mars is in its fall in Cancer, which rules the breasts. The brain is in the Aries part of the body, and since Mars rules Aries, a lack of B-12 causes deterioration of the brain and nerve cells.

Vitamin B-12 occurs in trace amounts in meats, and that is enough for good nutrition. The established daily requirement is 2 to 4 micrograms, but those with their Sun in Libra or Taurus may require somewhat larger quantities. Since a few vegetables supply adequate amounts of B-12, vegetarians are in danger of insufficiency unless they obtain it through dietary supplement. Absorption of B-12 is inhibited by excessive amounts of mucus in the small intestine, often caused by allergy to dairy products.

CHOLINE. Ruled by Jupiter, choline plays an essential role in the metabolism and distribution of fats. The body synthesizes this vitamin, but not in sufficient quantity, so additional amounts must be obtained through the diet. Inositol, also ruled by Jupiter, has much the same function as choline.

BIOTIN. Vitamin H, also Jupiter ruled, is essential in fat and protein metabolism and in maintaining proper chemical balance in the cells. Lack of biotin inhibits growth (Jupiter).

FOLIC ACID. This vitamin is ruled by Saturn. Mars is exalted in Saturn, and, as we might expect, folic acid is intimately related to vitamin B-12 and the formation of red blood cells. It is also important in protein metabolism, ruled by Saturn.

PANTOTHENIC ACID. As with many other Neptunian substances, the role of this vitamin in nutrition is somewhat obscure, but it is known to be important in the body's resistance to disease by helping in the production of antibodies. Pisces rules the lymphatic system, where these antibodies battle bacteria and viruses. Pantothenic acid is also thought to prevent graying of the hair, but this has not yet been clearly established.

PABA. Para-amino-benzoic acid, ruled by the Sun, is added to many sunscreen ointments to prevent sunburn. It is essential to growth and works with folic acid.

NIACIN. This vitamin, ruled by Venus, is absolutely essential to proper growth and to sugar metabolism (Venus ruled). Insufficient niacin affects the nervous system (Virgo, ruled by Mercury, is the fall dignity of Venus) and the brain (Aries is the detriment of Venus). In some persons, niacin, either as a supplement or in niacin-rich food, causes burning, flushing and itching. These are Mars ruled, and Scorpio is also the detriment of Venus. Most food supplements use the related vitamin niacinamide instead. The daily requirement is about 10 milligrams.

All of these latter vitamins in the B-complex group are found in the foods that are rich in the other B vitamins. All foods that contain these and other water-soluble vitamins should not be overcooked in water, because they dissolve in water.

In my opinion, this is probably the most important chapter in this book. I have pointed out that persons born under certain signs may need greater amounts of particular vitamins because of a hereditary inability to metabolize these compounds easily. The planetary ruler of the sign opposite your Sun sign indicates which vitamins you need to add to your diet. Aquarians, for example, require larger amounts of the Sun-ruled vitamins A and D, since the opposite sign, Leo, is ruled by the Sun.

I have frequently been asked if the sign opposite a person's rising sign indicates substances that the body metabolizes with greater difficulty. My own and other people's observations fail to confirm this. The Sun indicates a person's basic vitality, and the sign opposite the Sun sign indicates the greatest area of weakness.

Another point that needs further investigation is worthy of note in this discussion. The sign and the house that the Moon occupies in the horoscope indicate an individual's greatest need. It may well be that we have a greater need for those nutritional substances ruled by the planet that rules the Moon's sign. These substances could be vitamins, minerals, cell salts, carbohydrates, fat or protein. From personal observation, I am strongly inclined to believe that this is so, but I cannot prove it.

The house location of the Sun should not be overlooked either. The Sun in the first house almost always indicates a strong constitution and vitality. If your Sun is located here, the need for vitamins related to the sign opposite your Sun sign is probably minimized, whereas if your Sun is in the sixth or the twelfth house, the need for these substances is probably maximized.

A good rule in preparing food is to avoid, as much as possible, boiling foods that are rich in water-soluble vitamins and avoid frying foods that are rich in oil-soluble vitamins. Quite obviously, eating foods raw keeps the vitamins at their highest level. This is especially true of all foods rich in vitamin C, which is so easily destroyed upon standing.

As a rule, Americans are not very interested in proper diet planning, except possibly those born under Virgo. Quick meals are increasingly popular with the American public, especially foods fried in deep fat, which removes the oil-soluble vitamins A, D and E and increases the amount of cholesterol. However, our culture places a high premium on youthful appearance and physical beauty. A paradox. If you value youthful vigor and vitality and want to look far younger than you are, you will pay heed to this astrological lesson. It's up to you!

10

MINERALS AND
CELL SALTS

Thus far we have discussed those essential substances in our diet that are derived from living sources—chemical substances manufactured by other animals or by plants. However, while eating these organic substances, we also ingest certain inorganic compounds that have as their source the mineral kingdom.

Plants draw inorganic substances from the soil through their roots, and if the soil does not have enough of these compounds, the plant will not thrive. This is why we fertilize growing plants—to provide the essential minerals in sufficient quantity. In order for plants to grow, inorganic substances such as nitrate, phosphate or phosphorus, potash or potassium, and calcium must be present in the soil, along with trace amounts of many other minerals. Animals derive their minerals from plants, either directly or indirectly. Herbivores eat plants and thus get their minerals directly, while carnivores derive them from the flesh of the plant-eating animals that they eat.

Man, an omnivore, eats both plant and animal foods and obtains the essential minerals from both sources. As we learn more about nutrition, we are finding that it is sometimes necessary to supplement the minerals derived from natural sources. One reason is that man cooks many of his foods, both meat and plant, and in so doing often removes a considerable portion of the essential minerals, most of which are water-soluble. (They cannot be absorbed by the roots of the plant unless they are soluble in water.) When food is boiled, some of the minerals are dissolved in the boiling water and then discarded. Is it little wonder that nutritionists urge us to eat vegetables raw in salads, and when they must be boiled, to not overcook them?

I have already pointed out that the body manufactures enzymes from vitamins, but many enzymes also have an essential mineral component. Hemoglobin, the red substance in red blood corpuscles, must have the mineral iron, for example. Chemists call the raw materials from which the body manufactures essential chemicals "precursors." Both vitamins and minerals are precursors of enzymes. For the best health, then, one's daily diet must include a sufficient supply of minerals to replace worn-out enzymes in each cell.

Composition of Minerals

In their natural state, minerals have two basic components, a positively charged part and a negatively charged part. The positively charged component is usually a metal; the negatively charged part generally contains oxygen and some other nonmetallic substance.

When we say that the body needs phosphorus every day, we are really saying that it needs some form of mineral phosphate, such as calcium phosphate. Phosphorus does not exist alone in nature. It is the negatively charged part of a mineral molecule and is always attached to a metal such as sodium, potassium or calcium. Phosphate, essential to bone formation, is really a combination of phosphorus and oxygen. And when the body absorbs the phosphate, it also absorbs the metal to which the phosphate is joined.

Some minerals that we eat are only barely soluble in water. In digestion in the stomach, the insoluble mineral reacts with the strong acid called hydrochloric acid and is converted into a mineral form that is more soluble in water and therefore more easily absorbed. Remember, in order for digestion to take place in the small intestine, the substance must be water soluble.

There are twelve combinations of metal with nonmetal that the body can readily absorb without this reorganization process in the stomach. These compounds are called the physiological cell salts, and each one is in a form that the body can absorb directly without any intermediate reaction. The more chemically pure these substances are, that is, not contaminated by less soluble minerals, the more readily they are absorbed by the body. The cell salts have been isolated and identified as constituents of almost every body cell. However, the different cells have very specialized functions, and the proportions of the cell salts vary according to the cell's functions. The cell salts are discussed in more detail later in this chapter.

The Metallic Minerals

Certain metallic elements that the body requires for proper growth and nutrition must be included in the daily diet. Other metallic substances, such as lead, mercury and cadmium, are not tolerated by the body. If they creep into our diets, they can totally destroy some essential enzyme system. Good nutrition therefore means including the essential metals in the diet and avoiding totally those metals that interfere with enzyme production.

Astrologically, each of these metals has a planetary ruler. Here a thorough knowledge of the natal horoscope can be singularly advantageous in ensuring that the body gets all, but not too much, of the metals it needs for good nutrition. We all have the same general nutritional needs, which are labeled by the Department of Agriculture as the minimum daily requirement (MDR). But because we all are a little bit different, our individual nutritional requirements are also different.

As with vitamins, any mineral that is ruled by the planet that rules the sign opposite your Sun sign is one that your body is not equipped to metabolize readily. Thus you must add more of this mineral to your diet to ensure good nutrition.

Take, for example, a person whose Sun is in Cancer. The opposite sign is Capricorn, ruled by Saturn, which also rules calcium. This individual requires extra calcium for balanced nutrition. But in order for the body to properly absorb the calcium, that person must also have more of the minerals ruled by the Moon, which rules Cancer. The Moon rules fluoride, a nonmetal, and the Cancer person might well supplement his diet with a small amount of fluoride. However, too much fluoride can be poisonous to the system and cause mottling or spotting of the teeth. The proper balance is all-important. In many areas the drinking water contains sufficient fluoride to satisfy this requirement. Where it is not, a cup of tea every day is all that is needed, since tea contains fluoride. Many authorities now feel that excess fluoride in the diet may cause cancer.

As a basic rule of good nutrition, it is well to supplement your diet with foods that supply the basic mineral requirement rather than taking mineral supplements. Learn what foods contain the minerals ruled by the planetary ruler of the sign opposite your Sun sign. You'll benefit by including those foods in your daily diet, for they also contain the complementary minerals ruled by the planetary ruler of your Sun sign.

Briefly, let's look at some of the essential metallic minerals and their planetary rulers.

CALCIUM builds and maintains bones and teeth, helps blood to clot, aids vitality and endurance, regulates heart rhythm and is absolutely essential to good skeletal development. Insufficient calcium can cause rickets in growing children. It is ruled by Saturn.

IRON is required in the manufacture of hemoglobin, and it helps carry oxygen in the blood. Iron is ruled by Mars.

MAGNESIUM activates many enzyme systems, is essential in the metabolism of calcium and vitamin C and in the normal functioning of the nervous and muscular systems. It is ruled by the Sun.

COPPER is necessary for the proper absorption and

utilization of iron. It also helps form healthy red blood cells. Copper is ruled by Venus.

ZINC helps in the formation of tissue and is essential in protein and carbohydrate metabolism. It is ruled by Uranus.

MANGANESE activates various enzymes and is necessary for proper utilization of vitamins B-1 and E. It is ruled by the Sun.

COBALT stimulates the production of red blood cells. It is a component of vitamin B-12 and is necessary for normal growth and appetite. It is ruled by Mars.

POTASSIUM is necessary for healthy muscle tone and use. It affects the action of the heart and the nerves and many enzyme reactions. It is ruled by the Moon.

MOLYBDENUM is essential in proper carbohydrate metabolism. It is ruled by Venus.

The poisonous metals mercury, ruled by Mercury; lead, ruled by Saturn; arsenic, ruled by Mars; silver, ruled by the Moon; and cadmium, ruled by the Sun, are also present in our environment and can get into our food if we do not take proper precautions. Auto exhaust emits lead, which can be taken in by breathing. Insecticides on food may contain arsenic or mercury. Cadmium, sometimes used in glazes on pottery, can contaminate food eaten from the pottery. These metals are poisonous to the body, principally because they destroy certain enzyme systems in the cells. And of course, when enzyme systems are destroyed, the cell is destroyed.

The Nonmetallic Minerals

Along with the metals listed above, the body also requires a number of nonmetallic substances as well. Although only minute quantities of these minerals are necessary, a lack of one of them can be disastrous to good health. There are four principal nonmetallic minerals that are essential—phosphorus, iodine, sulfur and fluoride.

PHOSPHORUS is important for normal bone and tooth

structure, essential in energy production and use and related to the metabolism of calcium and of vitamin D. It is ruled by Mars.

IODINE is necessary for proper functioning of the thyroid gland. It is essential for proper growth, energy and regulation of the metabolism rate. It is ruled by the Sun.

SULFUR is vital to healthy skin, hair and fingernails. It is ruled by Jupiter.

FLUORIDE is required only in trace amounts, but it plays an important role in the formation of sound, healthy teeth and bones. It is ruled by the Moon.

A striking example of the effect of a lack of one of these minerals is insufficient iodine in the diet, which results in goiter, an enlargement of the thyroid gland. Lack of iodine slows down the rate of metabolism and causes listlessness. In a growing child, lack of iodine can impair the ability to learn and can actually contribute to mental retardation. The richest natural source of iodine is seafood, and since the early part of the twentieth century, iodine has been added to table salt to make up for the lack of natural iodine, especially in the diet of those who live far from the ocean.

Today the major controversy centers around the addition of fluoride to drinking water. Much of the drinking water in the United States contains fluoride naturally and so does not require fluoridation. Despite many advertising claims to the contrary, extra fluoride seems to be important only for children whose permanent teeth are still growing. Several recent studies indicate that excess fluoride in the diet is carcinogenic (cancer-causing). Fluoridation would be unnecessary if parents made sure that their children drank at least one cup of tea every day. Tea contains enough fluoride to aid in the development of strong, healthy teeth.

If you choose to add a mineral supplement to your diet, either metal or nonmetal, you should take it at the same time that you take your vitamins. Taking vitamins without minerals can be wasteful, since the body requires an adequate supply of both at the same time. The best time to take vitamin and mineral supplements is just before, during, or after meals. Between meals, the body is less able to absorb these substances.

One other word of caution. Two forms of iron are currently offered in mineral supplements—ferrous (iron) sulfate and chelated iron. Many doctors still prescribe ferrous sulfate tablets for pregnant women to ensure the health of both mother and unborn child. But ferrous sulfate tends to deactivate vitamin E, so the two should not be taken at the same time. Ferrous sulfate is an oxidizing agent, vitamin E is a deoxidant, and together these compounds negate each other's effect on the body. Chelated iron does not have this effect and may be taken at the same time as vitamin E.

Medical astrological research tells us that we require larger amounts of those vitamins and minerals that are related to the planet that rules the sign opposite the Sun sign. A person with a Scorpio Sun, for example, would require larger amounts of copper, molybdenum, vitamin E and niacin (vitamin B), either in the diet or through supplements. Taurus is the sign opposite Scorpio, and Taurus is ruled by Venus, which rules these substances. This principle also applies to the cell salts.

The Physiological Cell Salts

As mentioned earlier, the twelve basic physiological cell salts are combinations of a metal and a nonmetal in a form that is particularly easy for the body to absorb. They have been prescribed by practitioners and doctors of homeopathic medicine for many years, principally in England and Europe, as an aid in maintaining good health. The American public is just now beginning to recognize their value as a daily food supplement.

The cell salts are *not* drugs. They are very highly purified compounds of naturally occurring minerals that are normal constituents of the body cells. They are found in trace amounts in foods, because both plants and animals require these compounds for proper nutrition. And like the vitamins, cell salts get used up in the complex chemical reactions of each cell.

Therefore they must be constantly replenished in order to maintain healthy cells and tissues.

As explained in Chapter Seven, in order for each chemical reaction to take place, a particular enzyme must be present. Although the enzyme does not enter into the reaction, it does wear out and must be continually replaced. Enzymes are manufactured from vitamins and minerals, so lack of an essential vitamin or mineral means that certain enzymes cannot be replaced. This alters the normal cell chemistry, resulting in disease or malnutrition.

Disease conditions are also caused by other factors, of course. When the body fights disease, there is a greater demand on certain tissues, which speeds up their chemistry, resulting in a need for more vitamins and minerals to replace the worn-out enzymes. Any kind of tension or stress on some portion of the body makes the cell chemistry speed up. For example, long hours of concentrated study causes mental exhaustion because of added stress on the nerve tissues of the brain and eyes. When the body has a good reserve of the materials needed to replace the enzymes of these nerve cells, the feeling of tiredness disappears more rapidly.

The body's tissues and cells are highly specialized and require differing proportions of the cell salts. Thus when a disease occurs in some body tissue, an extra supply of the cell salts used by that tissue helps restore good health faster. For this reason you should take more of that specific salt.

The cell salts also are used by the endocrine glands to produce hormones, which are the body's chemical messengers, as I pointed out in Chapter Eight. An undersupply of any hormone poses a serious threat to the body and to life itself. Lack of insulin, for example, if untreated, can very quickly cause death. Thus there must be a reservoir of the essential minerals in the bloodstream to supply these ductless glands. The cell salts continually restock this reservoir. Also, at puberty there is a greater need for cell salts because of the increased production of sex hormones.

Because of individual variations in metabolism, people's requirements for the different cell salts vary. Some people need more of some than others do, which is largely a function of the times of conception and birth. Whether there is a cause and effect relationship between the cosmic field surrounding the earth and the hereditary pattern established at conception (and thus in hormonal activity), I leave to the reader to judge. In any case, in prescribing cell salts, the naturopathic healer refers to the person's horoscope to establish which ones are required in greater amounts.

Naturopathic medicine is a different kind of medicine than that commonly practiced in the United States. Most American doctors practice allopathic medicine, in which comparatively massive doses of certain chemicals, called drugs, are administered to alter the body chemistry and thus alleviate or cure the symptoms of the abnormal or disease condition. These drugs are foreign to the normal chemistry of the body in that they are not normally found in or produced by the body naturally.

By contrast, the naturopathic physician uses minute amounts of chemically pure substances that are natural to the body. His goal is to add just the right amount of those natural substances that will restore the body's healthy balance. The cell salts fall into this category of natural substances.

A Word of Caution

The cell salts are natural food material, not drugs. When used properly, they are no more dangerous than the vitamin and mineral supplements that Americans take every day. But they are not a cure-all, and they should not be considered a substitute for competent medical attention when disease conditions occur. There is an old and very wise axiom that, "He who treats himself has a fool for a patient." Do not think of the cell salts as drugs but as natural substances that help prevent disease and maintain good health.

People with serious chronic conditions, especially those related to the heart, should consult their physicians before beginning a daily regimen of cell salts. This is also true for any woman during pregnancy. It is, in fact, a good idea to ask your physician if there is any reason why you should not take cell salts or vitamins, for that matter. And if you are being treated by a physician, you should tell him about any dietary supplements that you are taking.

One other principle should be kept firmly in mind when using the cell salts to prevent disease—taking too large a dose does no good at all. Americans tend to believe that if some is good, more is better, but that is *not* true with cell salts. While healthy cells require a given amount of each of the cell salts, more than that amount can actually interfere with the functioning of that cell. Too much calcium salt, for example, can actually contribute to bone growths, sometimes called bone spurs, which must be removed surgically. Remember, too much can be just as harmful as not enough! If you have a specific disease, however, the cells usually require larger amounts of the cell salts to restore their normal function.

The Daily Regimen

Each of the twelve basic cell salts is traditionally assigned to one of the twelve zodiac signs (see Table I). Each one is a mineral salt of the highest purity in a form that can be absorbed directly into the system without any intermediate digestive process. I have mentioned that individuals differ in their needs for particular vitamins and minerals. This also applies to the cell salts. Table I shows which cell salts are most important for each of the twelve Sun signs. Another basic principle to keep in mind is that the assimilation of any cell salt is enhanced when it is accompanied by the Pisces cell salt, ferrum phos. Every dose of cell salts should include some ferrum phos.

The cell salts are known by their traditional Latin chemical names. For example, ferrum phos. stands for iron phosphate; kali mur. for potassium chloride; and nat sulph. for sodium sulfate. When you purchase these salts, you should ask for them by their Latin name. Cell salts may be purchased at any homeopathic pharmacy as well as at an increasing number of health food stores, for the public is becoming more aware of their value. In comparison to the usual prices for drugs and vitamins, the cell salts are relatively inexpensive.

Table I

Cell Salts for Each of the Zodiac Signs

Aries	Kali Phos and Nat. Phos.
Taurus	Nat. Sulph and Calc. Sulph.
Gemini	Kali Mur. and Silica
Cancer	Calc. Fluor. and Calc. Phos.
Leo	Mag. Phos. and Nat. Mur.
Virgo	Kali Sulph. and Ferrum Phos.
Libra	Nat. Phos. and Kali Phos.
Scorpio	Calc. Sulph. and Nat. Sulph.
Sagittarius	Silica and Kali Mur.
Capricorn	Calc. Phos. and Calc. Fluor.
Aquarius	Nat. Mur. and Mag. Phos.
Pisces	Ferrum Phos. and Kali Sulph.

The cell salts are dispensed in tiny tablets that dissolve almost immediately in the salivary juices of the mouth. They are best taken without water to aid in swallowing them; in fact, *they should not be swallowed at all.* Place the tiny tablets directly under your tongue and let them dissolve. This will happen almost immediately, with no unpleasant taste. They have hardly any taste at all. Because these salts are of such high purity and potency, they should not be mixed with other foods.

Cell salt tablets should be taken on an empty stomach thirty minutes before each meal and thirty minutes before bedtime—four times a day in divided doses. However, many people find that three times a day—thirty minutes before each meal—is more convenient, and that is all right too. For maximum benefit, a good multivitamin from natural sources should be taken at least once a day along with the cell salts. It is an accepted nutritional principle that vitamins should be taken along with the essential minerals, for as previously pointed out, *both* are required for the manufacture of enzymes. Turning this principle around, you can see that when taking cell salts, you should take your vitamin supplement at about the same time, with your meals.

Authorities differ somewhat about the correct dosage of cell salts, just as doctors and nutritionists differ as to the daily requirements for vitamins. However, the following regimen is quite widely accepted as adequate for good health. Four times a day, take the following dose: two ferrum phos. tablets and two each of the two cell salts listed for your sign in Table I. In other words, each dose consists of six tablets.

Once you've started your daily cell salt regimen, stick to it. They are not "wonder drugs," despite certain claims made by overzealous manufacturers. Don't expect wonders to happen overnight; there won't be any noticeable change for several weeks. But by sticking to your daily regimen, in the long run you should experience a feeling of greater well-being. Minor ailments may even diminish or disappear entirely, if their cause was related to an insufficient supply of cell salts.

Cell Salts for Minor Ailments

Naturopathic physicians have for many years prescribed additional amounts of certain cell salts, to be added to the daily regimen, for certain minor ailments. Following is a list of the physiological uses of each of the cell salts, together with the common ailments that each one seems to help. We make no claims for the efficacy of these suggestions; this is just a summary of the current cell salt literature.

I will repeat that there is no substitute for competent medical attention to the symptoms of ill health. Often such symptoms are indicative of a serious medical problem that should be brought to your physician's attention. However, many doctors do not object to the use of cell salts in addition to the drugs that they prescribe. But if you are taking any prescription medications, you ought to tell your doctor that you are also taking cell salts.

KALI PHOS. Potassium phosphate is the Aries cell salt. Its principal effect is reported to be on the nerve cells, especially the brain cells. It unites with the protein called albumin and with oxygen to form the "gray matter" of the brain. This salt is both healing and antiseptic. It is required for cell growth and cell reproduction. Kali phos. is used to treat all forms of mental fatigue, depression, insomnia, hysteria and headache. Because of its antiseptic properties, it is reported to be effective in treating certain skin conditions, especially when there is irritation or burning. It helps clean the pores and bathe the skin in protective oils and may be effective in the treatment of acne. Kali phos. is reportedly the most potent of all the cell salts. It is always taken with ferrum phos.

NAT. SULPH. Sodium sulfate is the principal Taurus cell salt. This is the first salt to be used up when a person born under Taurus becomes ill. Its chief function is reported to be the elimination of excess fluid from the body. Nat. sulph. has the property of chemically attracting large volumes of water. It is said to be especially important in the digestive process for production of bile and pancreatic juice and for proper kidney functioning. It is reportedly given for gall and kidney stones, jaundice and constipation. It is said to reduce swelling and other edamatous conditions, such as swelling that occurs after an injury or sprain.

KALI MUR. Potassium chloride, the Gemini cell salt, is important in the formation of most cells except bone cells and helps the cells retain their form. Kali mur. enables the body to assimilate other nutritional substances from food, and insufficiency is said to result in weight loss and malnutrition. It is given with ferrum phos. to relieve inflammation and irritation as well as in all respiratory problems such as colds, hay fever or postnasal drip. Sore throat, tonsilitis, swollen glands and many childhood diseases such as measles, chicken pox and scarlet fever are also reportedly helped by the administration of kali mur. It also seems helpful in treating dry and scaling skin conditions like dandruff and psoriasis. When used with silica, it is reportedly helpful in reducing pitting after chicken pox or acne, and it helps reduce formation of scar tissue in burns.

CALC. FLUOR. Calcium fluoride is the Cancer cell salt. It is an important constituent of hard tissues like teeth, bones, fingernails and the lens of the eye and of the elastic fibers in muscle tissue. Its deficiency is said to cause these tissues to lose their elasticity. The most obvious indicator of insufficient calc. fluor. is the appearance of open cracks or fissures in the skin folds, as between fingers and toes, in the anus, corners of the mouth and behind the ears. It has been reported to be effective in the treatment of hemorrhoids, varicose veins, receding gums, loose teeth, cataracts and blurred vision, bony lumps and even in hardening of the arteries and valvular heart disease. Calc. fluor. is always administered with silica, for these two salts seem to work together. Some homeopaths prescribe this salt for expectant mothers, as it is said to make abdominal tissues more supple for easier delivery and to prevent sagging of the abdomen after delivery and of the breasts following breast feeding. However, it should never be used during pregnancy except on the advice of a physician.

MAG. PHOS. Magnesium phosphate is the Leo cell salt. It is associated principally with the motor and sensory nerves that carry impulses to and from the brain. Since the sensory nerves transmit pain, it is called the "anti-pain" salt and is reportedly effective in relieving headache, even migraine. It has a soothing and relaxing effect on the body and is said to relieve nervous tension. It is a well-accepted medical fact that insufficient magnesium can cause convulsions and muscular spasms. It is sometimes effective in relieving nervous constipation. Mag. phos., kali phos. and ferrum phos. are taken in rotation for practically all forms of tiredness and exhaustion from overwork, insomnia, spasm, cramps and neuralgia. In this regimen the naturopath prescribes kali phos. with meals, ferrum phos. after meals and mag. phos. in the morning, afternoon and before bedtime.

KALI SULPH. Potassium sulfate is the Virgo cell salt. It helps primarily in the manufacture and distribution of oily secretions in the skin and hair. The skin secretions keep the pores open, which aids in perspiration and elimination of poisons. Insufficient kali sulph. can cause clogging of the pores and buildup of these toxins in the skin. Thus it is effective in the treatment of skin conditions, especially acne. Kali sulph. is also an important constituent of hair and scalp and is said to minimize dandruff and falling hair. It carries oxygen to the skin cells and thus is reportedly effective in minimizing scar tissue formation and in maintaining young-looking skin. It works particularly well in combination with vitamin E. Kali sulph. can be thought of as the lubricant that keeps the body machinery working. It is said that a lack of sufficient kali sulph. causes a person to feel very uncomfortable and suffocated in an overheated room, especially in the afternoon.

NAT. PHOS. Sodium phosphate is the cell salt needed most by those born under Libra. Its function is to maintain the body's acid-base balance by preventing excess acidity or alkalinity, especially in the bloodstream. It aids the kidneys in their function. Overacidity can cause coma and collapse. In order for all of the other cell salts to work properly, this acid-base balance must be maintained. Since it relieves excess acidity, nat. phos. has been used to treat gout, kidney stones, tired muscles, ulcers and acid stomach. Insufficient nat. phos. is said to produce a characteristic yellow coating of the tongue.

CALC. SULPH. Calcium sulfate is the Scorpio cell salt. It is an important constituent of the cells of all connective tissue and is absolutely essential in all healing processes. All of the sulph. salts have a purifying effect on the body. Calc. sulph. is nature's cleanser and purifying agent and, used with molasses, is a well-known oldtime home remedy. This salt prevents the gastric juices from dissolving the stomach lining, and thus it has been used to treat ulcers. A deficiency of this salt usually causes stomach problems, and since it is also important in forming the reproductive hormones, lack of it affects the ovaries, testes and prostate gland. In combination with other cell salts, it is used to relieve constipation. Whenever something must be eliminated from the body, calc. sulph. is reported to be effective.

SILICA.   Silicon dioxide is the Sagittarius cell salt. Seen under the microscope, its crystals are sharply pointed, which leads some naturopaths to call this salt "nature's knife." Silica is an important constituent of glass, so it should not be surprising to learn that it is an important constituent of the lens of the eye and necessary for good vision. It also gives the bones, fingernails and hair a more glossy appearance, especially the teeth. Its tiny sharp crystals help keep the skin pores open. Taking silica after surgery helps minimize scar tissue formation. The body requires only a trace amount of silica to maintain good health, but without it the fingernails become more brittle and the teeth more susceptible to tooth decay. It is complementary to the Cancer salt, calc. fluor., and these two are often administered together.

CALC. PHOS.   Calcium phosphate, the Capricorn salt, is a very important constituent of bone tissue. The body requires larger amounts of this cell salt than of all the others, especially during childhood growth or when recovering from broken bones. It is an essential part of the digestive juices and without sufficient calc. phos., food may pass through the digestive tract without releasing its nutritional elements. This salt has an important role in the clotting mechanism of the blood, and an insufficiency can mean that the blood takes longer to clot, resulting in hemorrhage. Bright's disease is said to be related to lack of this cell salt, as are skeletal problems such as rickets, curvature of the spine, tooth problems and decay. Rheumatism, arthritis and swollen or painful joints, such as bursitis, are reportedly helped by an extra dose of calc. phos. every day. It works in complement with kali phos., and the two are normally administered together.

NAT. MUR. Sodium chloride, the Aquarius salt, is chemically identical to common table salt, but in a much more highly purified state. Its uses as a preservative and as a seasoning have been known since ancient times. Fruits and vegetables are good natural sources of this salt. It is found in every body cell and fluid, where one of its most important roles is to preserve the correct fluid tension (osmotic pressure) in the cells and thus help them retain their shape. Its primary function is to transport fluids to areas of the body where they are required. Symptoms of insufficient nat. mur. are associated with watery conditions, such as watery colds, dropsy, dryness of the mouth, constipation, shingles and slowed healing of insect bites. Lack of this salt is said to cause insomnia, because the brain tissue is too dry. Too much water in the brain tissue may cause a heavy, tired and drowsy feeling. Upon awakening you feel more tired than when you went to bed. Nat. mur. is reportedly helpful in treating blisters, swelling, itching, eczema, redness and burning of the skin, as in sunburn. A paste of nat. mur., kali mur., calc. sulph. and ferrum phos. applied to the skin is said to be effective in the relief of skin problems and itching from insect bites. Except for calc. phos., we need more nat. mur. than the other salts.

FERRUM PHOS. Iron phosphate, the Pisces salt, is the only common metal salt among the twelve cell salts, and its importance in making all of the other cell salts more effective has already been mentioned. It is required for healthy red blood cells, and lack of it can cause anemia. Its most important function is to distribute oxygen to all of the body tissues, which is especially important when the body is fighting off infection. Insufficient oxygen means that all basic body processes slow down; thus the lack of ferrum phos. can cause the individual to tire more quickly. This salt is reportedly essential in treating many afflictions because it supplies the increased oxygen needed by the afflicted tissues. Thus it shortens the period of convalescence and promotes more rapid healing. All living cells require oxygen to produce the energy for all of their chemical reactions, so you can see why this salt is especially important.

11

THE NODAL CHART

Mundane astrology provides us with a number of supplemental charts that can be used with the natal chart to more clearly understand, and thus delineate, the natal chart, and also to time events. These charts are the lunar and solar return charts, the various types of progressed charts, the solar conversion chart and the relocation chart.

A technique that is often used by older and more traditional astrologers is to place the planet being studied on the first house cusp and, using its longitude degrees and minutes, set up an equal house chart, much as one might construct a solar chart when the birthtime is unknown. After all of the other planets are placed in the chart by proper longitude location, the chart is delineated in the usual manner by house and aspect to the planet on the Ascendant. One such chart, called a nodal chart, is of particular importance to the medical astrologer.

In his excellent book *Karmic Astrology*, Martin Schulman says, "It is generally accepted in the astrological community today that the nodes of the Moon represent the major key toward understanding your life as part of a continual thread. Many astrologers believe that the nodes hold more importance than the rest of the chart. To a qualified expert, a knowledge of the Sun, Moon and nodal positions can reveal the entire life of the individual." Unfortunately I cannot completely agree that the nodes are as widely accepted as he suggests, but I do agree most emphatically that a qualified expert can understand a person's health from the Sun, Moon and nodal positions. The nodal chart at least can point up potential health problem areas that can be protected in a good program of preventive medicine.

The Ascendant represents the point in time when the physical body enters life as an independent being. The South Node of the Moon represents the past; the North Node of the Moon represents the future. The nodal axis of the horoscope is like the needle of a compass, with the North Node as the tip, pointing the direction in which the soul must travel during this lifetime.

In the birth process, the crown of the skull usually emerges from the mother first; the feet are the last to emerge. As Schulman points out: "The potentially weakest spot in any horoscope is the South Node...." And the potentially weakest spot in a newborn baby is the top of the head, because it is still quite soft. A sharp blow to this area could result in instant death. When we move from one place to another, the first part of the body to reach and touch this place is the foot. When you move about in the dark, which part of the body do you protect most? The head.

Thus, in constructing this nodal chart, we place the South Node's position on the first house cusp, the Ascendant; we place the North Node's position on the seventh house cusp, the Descendant. The Ascendant represents the top of the head, and the Descendant, the soles of the feet. The horizontal axis connecting these two points represents the central axis of the body and also the spine. The center of the wheel does *not* represent the navel, as might be supposed, but rather what the Orientals refer to as the "kundalini point," the point of connection between the physical and etheric bodies. This point is about two or three inches below the navel. In the contemplative statues of Buddha, he is contemplating this point, not the navel.

In traditional astrology, the first six houses represent one's personal development, and the last six houses, one's participation in group life. The Sun, representing the individuality

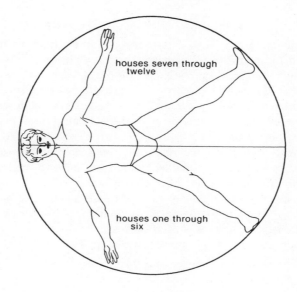

houses seven through
twelve

houses one through
six

Figure 2.   Areas of the body and the nodal chart.

and the ego, is linked most closely to personal development. The Moon, representing the public and external circumstances, is linked most closely to participation in the external environment. Traditional medical astrology links the Sun to the right side of the body and the Moon to the left side.

If we visualize the human body as lying face up on the nodal chart, with the head at the Ascendant and the feet at the Descendant along the horizontal axis (the horizon line), as shown in Figure 2, we can quickly see the proper anatomical correspondences. The first six houses represent the right side of the body, under the general rulership of the Sun; the last six houses represent the left side, under the general rulership of the Moon. The anatomical correspondences then fall into place as follows:

Houses twelve and one represent the head and neck with
the second and twelfth house cusps falling along the
axis of the collarbone.
Houses two and eleven represent everything in the chest

cavity from the collarbone to the diaphragm, including the heart, with the third and eleventh house cusps falling along the axis of the diaphragm.

Houses three and ten represent the stomach, upper small intestine, liver, spleen and pancreas, extending down to an imaginary line through the kundalini point just below the navel.

Houses four and nine represent the lower abdomen, rectum, kidneys, bladder, large intestine and organs of reproduction, as well as the hips.

Houses five and eight represent the buttocks and upper legs, extending down to an imaginary line drawn through the center of each kneecap.

Houses six and seven represent the lower legs and feet.

In each case, houses one through six represent the right side of the region; houses seven through twelve, the left side.

Interpreting the Nodal Chart

We are now ready to place each planet by sign location in the nodal chart, just as calculated in the natal horoscope. The house location of each planet in the nodal chart gives us the keys to its interpretation. In doing this, we must keep in mind the symbolism of the planets, as explained in Chapter Two. As you try this exercise with your own natal horoscope, I think you will be as startled and surprised as I and many of my students have been by the accuracy of this technique.

Let us see how each planet indicates potential or actual health problems.

THE SUN. The Sun is the expression of our individuality and in terms of "body language," the area of the nodal chart containing the Sun is often the most physically expressive part of the body. With a twelfth or first house Sun, the face (often the eyes) is the most expressive. With a second or eleventh house Sun, the hands are usually used freely in expression. With a sixth or seventh house Sun, tapping or crossing the feet or lower legs can be quite revealing of the person's personality. A fifth or eighth house Sun, especially in a woman, can telegraph a very definite "come hither" message.

The Sun's placement often indicates the area of the body that is most important to the individual's professional activity. For example, a fifth or eighth house placement is important for an athlete (upper legs); a twelfth or first house placement can indicate someone whose profession depends on thinking; and a sixth or seventh house placement may indicate a dancer. The Sun's placement also often indicates the part of the body that is used most. The Sun represents the father, and in many charts of individuals whose fathers have died, the Sun's house placement indicates the area of the father's body involved in the cause of death.

THE MOON.   The Moon represents the way in which we reach out to touch others emotionally. People with a second or eleventh house Moon tend to touch those to whom they are talking. It also represents the body fluids, and when the body does not handle fluids properly, they tend to accumulate in the area of the Moon's placement.

The Moon represents the mother, and in many charts of individuals whose mothers have died, the Moon's house placement indicates the area of her body most closely involved as the cause of death.

The nodal house of the Moon sometimes indicates the area of the body that requires or attracts our greatest attention, either for health or cosmetic reasons. It is frequently the most tender or sensitive area to pain or stimulation. Most persons with a twelfth or first house Moon particularly dread going to the dentist. Individuals with a fourth or ninth house Moon are highly sensitive and responsive during sexual intercourse.

MERCURY. Mercury is associated with the nervous system and also with what we tend to worry about most. Nervous problems, if there are any, tend to manifest in the body region associated with Mercury's nodal house placement. A right arm that is shaky after vigorous usage would be typical with Mercury in the second house. Also, one tends to worry most about the area of the body represented by Mercury's nodal house placement. This region gets more conscious attention. Malefic aspects to Mercury in the chart make this phenomenon more apparent.

VENUS. The region of the body occupied by Venus in the nodal chart is also quite sensitive to touch and stimulation; however, unlike the Moon, stimulation of this area tends to be more pleasure-producing. This region is often the most physically beautiful portion of the body, provided it is not heavily aspected by malefics. A twelfth or first house nodal placement of Venus makes one "fair of face"; a second or eleventh house placement of Venus greatly enhances a woman's figure.

Consciously or unconsciously, this region becomes very important during lovemaking, For an individual with a twelfth or first house Venus in the nodal chart, a kiss can be most meaningful and important. A hug or being held closely by one's partner is especially meaningful when Venus is in the second or eleventh nodal house. A malefic aspect from Saturn to Venus often creates the desire but at the same time a certain fear connected with this area—a desire to be kissed, for example, but at the same time a fear of closeness.

MARS. Mars plays a very important role in the nodal chart, and its house position and aspects must be examined very closely. Mars' house placement often indicates the area of the body most likely to be injured in an accident. Look for scars in this region. Frequency of accidents usually depends upon how Mars is aspected—the more malefic, the more accidents.

Mars, representing the muscular system, can signal the most muscularly developed area of the body. More important, however, the muscles in this area are most likely to become tense as a physical expression of mental tension. With good aspects to Mars, the tension is more easily relieved; hard aspects tend to increase this tension.

Because Mars represents inflammation and heat, its nodal

location can indicate the warmest part of the body. If Mars is adversely aspected by Pluto, this area can be the site of the most frequent bacterial and viral infections. If Mars is adversely aspected by the Moon, this can be the area of physical manifestation of allergy, as the Moon is associated with allergic reactions. Persons with a twelfth or first house Mars frequently have a particularly difficult time with acne in their teens, unless Mars is well aspected. A person is likely to require surgery on Mars' nodal region at some time; many with a nodal fourth house Mars have to have an emergency appendectomy.

JUPITER. "Jolly old Jupiter" symbolizes fat, and fat tends to accumulate most obviously in Jupiter's nodal region. This area of the body tends to be larger in proportion to the other areas. With a fourth or ninth house Jupiter, the middle-age paunch is common. A first or twelfth house Jupiter usually signals a rather large head; a sixth or seventh house Jupiter, big feet, etc. Jupiter also tends to protect this area of the body from harm; however, when that area is diseased, the problem is magnified.

Jupiter signifies overactivity, and its nodal zone is sometimes the area of the body that gets overused. People do not always recognize the physical limitations of this region and sometimes place excessive demands upon it, especially when both Jupiter and Mars are in the same region. For example, a first or twelfth house Jupiter may signal one who uses his mind to the point of exhaustion; often a person with Jupiter in the fourth or ninth house may have low back pain from trying to lift heavy objects or from using the wrong muscles in lifting.

Finally, Jupiter sometimes signals physiological overactivity in its nodal region. For example, persons with Jupiter in the first or twelfth may have an overactive thyroid gland or enlarged tonsils. Jupiter in the third or tenth would be classical for hypoglycemia.

SATURN. Saturn's nodal position is usually quite important for a number of reasons. Physically, this region tends to be underdeveloped or reduced in proportion to the rest of the body. Since Saturn rules hair, this area is frequently hirsute. Men with Saturn in the nodal first or twelfth usually have lots of head hair and are rarely bald. People with Saturn in the nodal second or eleventh often have thin or underdeveloped arms and/or chest, with lots of hair. If Saturn is retrograde, the hair is more on the upper back. With Saturn in the nodal fourth or ninth, the hips or waist tend to be narrower than normal. Saturn in the nodal sixth or seventh indicates thin ankles and small feet.

Saturn may signal underactivity or underdevelopment in its nodal region. For example, Saturn in the nodal first or twelfth often indicates impaired hearing or eyesight; an underactive thyroid or thymus gland; a very bony and angular head, which also tends to be rather small; in some cases retarded mental development or lowered intelligence; or reduced physical height because of Saturn's effect upon the pituitary gland. The onset of puberty may also be delayed for the same reason.

Persons who have arthritis often have the most pain and the greatest joint disfigurement in the area that corresponds to Saturn's location in the nodal chart. With Saturn in the eleventh or second house, we sometimes find congestive heart failure or emphysema. Persons with Saturn in the fifth, sixth, seventh or eighth house sometimes are subject to phlebitis, in which the blood flow is blocked in some part of the legs. Bone spurs sometimes tend to develop in Saturn's region. Blockage of fluid in some area is indicated when Saturn in that area is square or inconjunct the Moon.

URANUS. Earlier we linked Uranus to the involuntary nervous sytem, most likely to the sympathetic nerve trunk. Since Neptune rules the parasympathetic nerve trunk, each trunk controls the functions of the other, opposites again keeping each other under control. Uranus can indicate greater freedom for the area it represents in the nodal chart, but also a lack of coordination with the other body parts, which sometimes makes this area more subject to accidents. A nervous tic or involuntary twitch sometimes manifests in Uranus' region if Uranus is under tension aspects.

Uranus is traditionally associated with intuition, especially when it is in the twelfth or first house, where its effect on the brain is emphasized. With Uranus in the eleventh house or, especially, the second, we have the typical healer or person with healing hands.

NEPTUNE. Many psychologists and physical culturists say that people are out of touch with their physical bodies. Neptune's position in the nodal chart usually indicates the region with which we are most out of touch. Often pain is felt less severely here, or physical problems are overlooked for one reason or another. Diagnosing problems in this region becomes more difficult for the healer. Many people with Neptune in the nodal twelfth or first suffer from headache—migraine in particular—that is very difficult to diagnose and treat properly.

Neptune and Pisces rule the body's defense mechanisms, and when nodal Neptune is under tension aspect, its nodal house location often indicates the site of frequent infections, especially with Mars square Neptune. The Neptune region is where toxins tend to accumulate, especially in the lymphatic system. Drugs sometimes have unpredictable and undesirable side effects on this region, especially with Uranus square Neptune.

Neptune in the twelfth or first house affects the brain, and the individual is likely to have special extrasensory abilities, such as precognition. Neptune in the second or eleventh house can give the fingers an exquisite sense of touch, and this placement is found in the nodal charts of many musicians and magicians. Neptune tends to sharpen the senses, especially touch, in the region it occupies, while paradoxically deadening response to pain at the same time.

PLUTO. Pluto is most closely associated with the hereditary materials of the cell, and when Pluto is under tension aspect, cell reproduction may go awry. The result can be as simple as a wart or as dangerous as a malignancy. Often moles and birthmarks are found in Pluto's nodal area.

As we shall see in Chapter Eight, Pluto rules enzymes, and tension aspects to Pluto sometimes indicate problems with the enzyme systems that are in its nodal area. Infections are more common here also.

RETROGRADE PLANETS. Before proceeding further, I should point out that a retrograde planet affects the back portion of the region in which it is located more than the front portion. For example, a retrograde Pluto in the eleventh house would indicate that any abnormal growths would be on the left portion of the upper back; if Pluto is direct, such growths would be on the left upper chest.

As a general rule, if a planet in the nodal chart is located in the house that represents the organ ruled by that planet, it tends to give greater strength to the organ, allowing it to function more efficiently. For example, the Sun rules the heart, and when the Sun is in the second or eleventh nodal house, the heart is stronger and more efficient and is thereby better able to resist potential problems.

Right and Left Handedness

Several American astrological groups have recently attempted to use the natal chart to determine whether an individual is right or left handed. In most of the cases that I have discussed with them, their results have been rather inconclusive. I believe that research into handedness would be much more informative if the nodal chart were used.

First of all, we must accept the fact that right or left handedness is not a black or white situation, but rather a matter of the degree to which the individual favors one hand over the other. When the right hand is injured, some right-handed persons find it relatively easy to write with and use the left hand; others find it well-nigh impossible. We are all familiar with the switch-hitter in baseball who can bat right or left handed equally well. Some batters, however, are never able to master this.

Neurologists tell us that in right-handed persons the left side of the brain is more highly developed, and vice versa. This finding is confirmed in many cases by studying the nodal chart.

Generally, when the Sun is in the nodal twelfth house, representing the left side of the brain, the person is right handed. With the Sun in the nodal first house, representing the right side of the brain, the person is generally left handed or strongly inclined to use the left hand. Many with the Sun in either of these houses are ambidextrous.

When the Sun is in one of the other houses, we must see where the greater number of planets is located. A preponderance of planets in houses seven through twelve puts the emphasis on the left hand; a preponderance in houses one through six emphasizes the right hand. Planets almost equally distributed between these two shows the person's inclination to favor one hand or the other. A 5:5 distribution is classical for ambidexterity, usually with the side containing the Sun slightly favored over the other.

I would not want to have these rules quoted as some "scientific" finding, because I have never tested them in any scientific manner that would be acceptable to the medical profession. However, I have tested them tentatively on about 300 cases, and in better than 90 percent of these, the nodal chart correctly indicated handedness. While others interested in medical astrological research may well have discovered the value of the nodal chart as a diagnostic tool in delineation, I have not come across any report of their findings in the astrological literature to date. For this reason, I felt it necessary to report on my own findings, so that others might be stimulated to test out this technique and report on their results as well.

A Case Study

Now that we have examined the general principles of using a nodal chart as a supplementary aid in delineating for nutrition and health purposes, we will demonstrate with a particular case. Figure 3 shows an accurate natal horoscope with its corresponding nodal chart for a young woman, a college student in her mid-twenties, who began to experience quite a few health problems in early 1973 as the planet Saturn commenced its transit of her sixth house. Her symptoms were a marked loss of energy, dizziness to the point that on some days she could hardly get out of bed, and severe menstrual cramping. Her nutritional habits were quite poor, and with the onset of her problems she experienced anorexia (loss of appetite). She had visited several doctors and a chiropractor with little apparent improvement in her condition before turning to me as a friend for any suggestions that I might have.

Frankly, this is a difficult position for any astrologer. On the one hand, there is a desire to help a close friend in need, but on the other hand, it is illegal for an astrologer to play doctor and attempt to diagnose disease. Also, unless the astrologer is a medical doctor, which is quite rare these days, he must recognize the limitations of his medical and nutritional knowledge. How then can an astrologer be of service in such a situation? In order to answer this question, we must first examine her chart.

Her natal chart is in the almost classical locomotive pattern, with a Grand Water Trine (Mars retrograde, Venus and Uranus). Venus's position in the pattern shows that it is the planet in high focus. Uranus also assumes a position of special prominence because it is the center of focus of a cardinal T-Cross (Saturn retrograde/Sun + Mercury retrograde = Uranus). Note that Uranus participates in both the Grand Trine and the T-Cross and also rules the second house, which contains Venus. Saturn is the chart ruler, retrograde at birth, and thus its transits and progressions must be particularly watched for the timing of important events in this person's life.

As was discussed in Chapter Five, Venus rules sugar and carbohydrates. We have already noted that the second house indicates food preference. With Venus in the second house, this woman's diet had been exceptionally high in sugars and "junk food" (food high in sugar and starch, with very little other nutritional content). Aquarius on the cusp of this house usually indicates a strong preference for salt, and she was in the habit of salting almost all of her food.

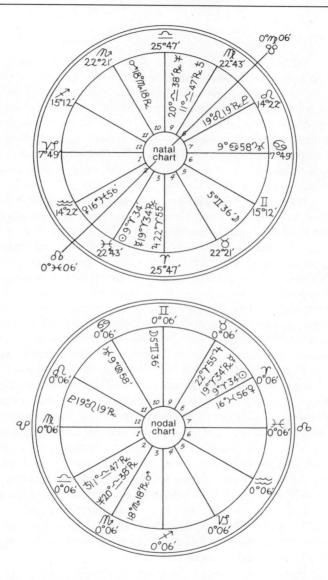

Figure 3.   Natal and nodal charts of a young woman, born
March 30, 1952, 1:11 A.M. MST, 106° W 30′, 31° N 45′

With Gemini on the cusp of the sixth house, mealtime was a time for pleasant conversation. Indeed, with Moon in Gemini, she enjoyed pleasant conversation at any time, and she believed that all emotional feelings must have some rational basis. Mercury rules the sixth house, and natally Mercury is opposed by Saturn as well as Neptune (note that all three are retrograde) from the ninth house. This configuration strongly suggests that the physical symptoms of disease are likely to have a mental basis.

How does this woman approach her problems? With Gemini on the cusp of the sixth house, her tendency sometimes is to "talk the problem to death" to avoid dealing with it. At other times, she pretends that the problem does not exist and thus will magically disappear. With Neptune opposing Mercury (and both retrograde), serious medical problems are obscured and therefore difficult to diagnose. With Uranus in her seventh house in a strongly emphasized position (coming from this Mercury opposed Saturn/Neptune T-Cross), she is inclined to ignore advice from doctors anyway. Remember that the seventh house represents a person whom we consult on a one-to-one basis.

Turning to the nodal chart for further information, we note that Pluto in Leo is retrograde in the twelfth house, representing the ears. Pluto also rules enzymes, and in this woman's family there is a history of lack of an important enzyme required for proper functioning of the nervous system. Venus is conjunct Pluto in Pisces, the sign ruled by Neptune, which would tend to obscure and make more difficult any Venus-related problems.

As Saturn left her sixth house and approached the seventh house and Uranus, the problem grew worse, then lessened as Saturn passed into Leo. Saturn's activation of the cardinal T-Cross through this transit over Uranus lowered her vitality considerably and at the same time caused the breakup of a close personal relationship.

Now I can answer my initial question—what advice should I give this woman, aside from recommending the proper glucose tolerance test? I suggested that she submit to a new battery of tests in order to determine whether the sugar metabolism problem is in fact caused by lack of some important enzyme (Venus inconjunct Pluto) or a hidden growth on the left side of the brain (Pluto in nodal twelfth). Because her case requires long-term study, I cannot report the final outcome at this time, but I feel that the Venus inconjunct Pluto symbolizes the cause of her problems in some way.

I would also like to comment on another significant point, which is that many astrologers fail to consider the importance of analyzing the planetary pattern in each chart that they examine. If I had not analyzed the pattern in this chart, I would have overlooked Venus' important position as the planet in high focus. The locomotive pattern led me right to the heart of the problem. I strongly recommend that every astrologer and student learn to recognize the various planetary patterns and their importance.

As a final postscript to this chapter, note that the planets in the nodal chart are distributed in the classical pattern for left handedness—Sun above the horizon and six other planets in houses seven through twelve, the left-hand side of the nodal chart.

In the last chapter of this book, I discuss the matters of birth and death in some detail, using the natal and nodal charts of President Lyndon B. Johnson as an example, according to the principles covered in this chapter. The results are very interesting and enlightening.

12

ELECTIVE SURGERY
AND TRANSITS

As far back as ancient times, there is considerable written evidence of attempts by astrologers to pick the most advantageous time for certain events, to ensure a positive outcome. Ptolemy, in his *Tetrabiblos,* establishes rules for determining the best time for such events as weddings, public ceremonies and festivals, attacks on one's enemies, the signing of legal documents and, certainly not least, surgery.

Perhaps the most common request that I, as a medical astrologer, receive from clients and students is to help them select a good date for elective surgery. Unfortunately, it is not usually possible to choose an advantageous time for emergency surgical procedures such as appendectomy, operation on a perforated ulcer or tracheotomy. However, doctors and hospitals usually allow the patient to choose in advance the date of elective surgery such as hernia repair, hemorrhoidectomy, tonsillectomy, circumcision, hysterectomy, gall-bladder operation or cosmetic surgery. Most hospitals do not, of course, permit a patient to choose the time of day for surgery.

While I fully believe that "he who treats himself has a fool for a patient," and that everyone should consult a recognized healing arts practitioner for health problems, I also feel that there is no moral or ethical reason why a professional astrologer, fully versed in the basic rules, should not help a client select the best date possible for elective surgery. Anyone who has a working knowledge of astrology, especially in reading an ephemeris, can easily apply the rules given here for selecting such a date. These rules are based not only on Ptolemy's directions, but also on reports published in current medical literature by doctors who are not astrologers.

The Lunar Influence

Probably the single most important factor in selecting a date for elective surgery is the sign that the Moon is in as it transits the zodiac and its position in relation to the person's natal chart. The lunar influence gives us some very definite do's and dont's for selecting a date for surgery. Perhaps the most important "don't" is: if possible, do not arrange to have surgery the day before, the day of or the day after the full Moon. Several recent nonastrological studies have shown strong evidence that there is increased danger of hemorrhage when surgery is performed at this time of the lunar month. This is because the surface tension of all fluids appears to be at its lowest level at this time, so that substances such as blood clots seem to be most likely to dissolve. A recent study by two surgeons who specialize in tonsillectomies, published in the prestigious *New England Journal of Medicine*, appears to bear out this theory.

This brings us to the interesting observation that many babies are born at or close to the full Moon. While there is still no statistical evidence of this phenomenon, over the years many nurses have assured me that they are inevitably most busy at the time of the full Moon. This makes good scientific sense, for if the fluid tension is lowest at this time, then the probability of release of the amniotic fluid should be increased, with parturition following soon after.

However, it is also fair to say that if this phenomenon is true, astrologers should see many clients whose natal Sun and Moon are in opposition, but this has not been my experience in over ten years of consultation with clients. Full-Moon births may be frequent, but my observations have not confirmed this.

Let us put to rest another old wives' tale, which states that babies born at the time of an eclipse are born dead. I have in my files a number of cases of persons born during or very close to a solar or lunar eclipse who have grown to adulthood and are quite normal in every respect. Pope Pius XII is said to have been born under such an eclipse, and he certainly lived long enough to enjoy a full and rewarding life!

Ptolemy suggests that surgery should *not* be performed when:

1.   The transiting Moon is in any sign ruling the vital organs, such as Leo, which rules the heart.

2.   The transiting Moon is in the Ascendant of the patient's natal horoscope, since this position decreases the vitality.

3.   The transiting Moon is in the sign ruling the part of the body that requires surgery. For example, one should not have an abdominal operation when the Moon is in Virgo or a head operation when the Moon is in Aries or a tonsillectomy when the Moon is in Taurus.

4.   Transiting Mars opposes the patient's natal Moon or when Mars is within 17° of the natal Sun. Both positions are said to decrease vitality and lengthen post-surgical recuperation.

The Solar Influence

The Sun represents your vitality or life force, and since vitality ideally ought to be at its peak during surgery, the position of the Sun is important when you are choosing a date for an operation.

Ptolemy states that the transiting Sun should not be in the sign that symbolizes the body region that requires surgery. For example, he suggests that hemorrhoidectomy should not be done while the Sun is in Scorpio and that chest surgery should not be performed while the Sun is in Gemini. At these times, surgery in those areas would be a greater drain on one's basic vitality, and the period of convalescence would be lengthened.

The better date for surgery would be when the transiting Sun is either sextile or trine the natal Sun and at the same time not in square or opposition to other planets, especially Mars or Saturn. Contraparallels may or may not have a similar effect.

The Influence of Mars

Mars is very important for any surgical procedure, since it symbolizes the surgeon's knife. Well aspected, Mars symbolizes protection during surgery and attainment of the desired result. If Mars is afflicted, especially by square or opposition from the Sun, Moon, Saturn or Neptune, there is reportedly danger of complications during or just after the operation.

The eighth house of the natal chart is in the natural house of Scorpio, which is co-ruled by both Pluto and Mars. Traditionally the eighth house has been called the house of surgery. While I have never seen any hard statistical evidence to bear this out, it has been my personal observation that at some time in their life, many persons undergo surgery when Mars is transiting their eighth house. In many cases I have also observed that Mars is in the eighth house in a solar return chart for the year of the operation.

Another interesting occurrence, which I have personally observed many times and which is confirmed by many other astrologers, is that if a person's natal Mars is within a degree of two of the Ascendant, he or she may have been born by surgical procedure, usually Caesarean section. This is not always the case, but it happens often enough that I always ask clients whose Mars is closely conjunct their natal Ascendant whether they were born by Caesarean section. Many times the answer is yes.

Mars does not go retrograde very frequently, but when it does, the ancient astrologer-priests recommend avoiding surgical procedures. As far as I can determine, their reasoning was that the surgery might have to be repeated later or that further surgery might be necessary to correct some problem resulting from the first operation. Keloiding (scarring) or herniation would be examples of such problems.

Other Considerations

Modern observers have assigned abnormal growths such as tumors, warts, birthmarks and moles to Pluto. This planet was not discovered until 1930, so we do not have the benefit of centuries of observation of it, as we have for the planets known to the ancients. However, modern astrology has, correctly I believe, called Pluto the ruler of the hereditary material in living cells. Pluto is the alpha and omega, the planet in symbolic control of the moment of conception, when one's hereditary makeup is determined, as well as the moment of death of the physical body. Pluto is also the ruler of bacteria and viruses, which are the sources of many diseases and infections. There is also a mounting body of biochemical evidence linking viruses to cancerous cell growths.

In selecting a date for surgery, I personally would want Pluto to be as free as possible from other planetary afflictions. But most especially, I would want a time when Mars makes no aspect at all to Pluto, in order to minimize the chances of postsurgical infection from bacteria or viruses.

The condition of the natal twelfth house, as well as any planets that are transiting it, must also be given close attention, for hospitals and the postsurgical recovery period in the hospital are ruled by this house. The twelfth house is also symbolic of pain and suffering; in a larger sense it represents all life experiences that we must go through alone, and pain is certainly one of these experiences. Paradoxically, the twelfth house also represents periods in life when we must place ourselves completely in someone else's hands and rely on others to serve us, which is the case when we are hospitalized.

Under ideal astrological conditions, the twelfth house should be free of any negative or afflicting influences. We know, for example, that Saturn has a delaying effect. Its presence in the twelfth house or in opposition to the ruler of the twelfth might be indicative of delayed recovery from illness or surgery. If the Moon, the ruler of body fluids, is in this house after surgery, it may indicate swelling. This would be even more likely if at the same time Jupiter is in square or opposition to the Moon, for Jupiter expands, and in a surgical situation this can mean swelling.

On the other hand, Venus in either the eighth or the twelfth house or in benefic aspect to the ruler of either of these houses should indicate a very favorable outcome of the surgery and rapid convalescence and healing. While most astrological textbooks treat Venus rather harshly when it is in the natal twelfth house, in medical astrology this position makes Venus a guardian angel, promoting rapid healing and deliverance from unknown enemies, including bacteria and other infectious organisms.

Neptune is another outer planet that the ancient astrologer-priests did not know of. Quite likely Neptune was the culprit when the king lost the battle that they predicted he would win! Neptune is a slow mover, and very often its effects cannot be eliminated at the time when surgery is to take place. It is no coincidence that Neptune was discovered in the 1800's at about the same time that anesthetics, like chloroform, ether and nitrous oxide, were discovered, since Neptune rules anesthetics as well as artificial drugs and chemical poisons. Neptune masks the symptoms of disease and so can deceive the medical diagnostician. Those persons whose natal Neptune is in either the sixth or the twelfth house should probably seek out several medical opinions before undergoing surgery or treatment of a severe medical problem. Even with Neptune in benefic sextile aspect to Pluto, as in the horoscope of most persons born in the latter half of the twentieth century, cancerous growths, with their poisonous toxins, often go undiscovered and undiagnosed until it is too late to solve the problem. Even without the keen insights of the ancient astrologer-priests, we can say that it would be wise, based on what we now know of Neptune, to select a date for surgery when Neptune's effects on the natal chart are minimal or at least unrelated to the planets symbolizing the surgical condition to be corrected.

This discussion would certainly not be complete without some consideration of Jupiter, which in terms of medical astrology is highly overrated. This planet truly presents a mixed bag as to position and aspects at the time of surgery. When transiting the twelfth house, Jupiter can be highly beneficial, provided it is not badly aspected at and following the date of surgery. Badly aspected, Jupiter can expand or extend the recovery period. In aspect to the planet that symbolizes the condition being treated, it can expand the condition. For example, little tumors grow rapidly (Jupiter square Pluto), tiny gallstones rapidly increase in size (Jupiter square Saturn), minor surgery becomes major (Jupiter square Mars). Natal Jupiter within a degree or two of the Ascendant usually indicates a baby that is unusually large at birth; I've seen several who were over ten pounds.

On the other hand, when Jupiter is in good aspect to the Sun at the time of surgery, the recovery period can be very rapid, because the vitality is very high at this time. When transiting the third house, Jupiter can affect the patient's mental attitude very positively, which also speeds recovery. However, if it is negatively aspected at this time, the patient may expect too much from the surgical procedure.

The third house of the natal chart should be considered when deciding on a date for surgery, for it reveals the patient's mental attitude. The mind is a wondrous thing, and its state during and after surgery can minimize or prolong the period of recovery. Many doctors now feel that perhaps three-quarters of the physical diseases of patients in hospitals are caused by negative mental states. For this reason, the status of the third house probably should be given prime consideration in selecting a date for surgery.

Choosing a Healer

Synastry, one of the oldest astrological arts, is the art of understanding human relationships through a comparison of the natal charts of the persons involved. It is certainly one of the most popular courses taught today in the astrological field. Alas, most students are so preoccupied with finding the right mate that they have forgotten that the rules of synastry apply equally to selecting a doctor or dentist!

A complete treatment of synastry would require a whole book, and I have covered this subject in another book: *Synastry—The Art of Chart Comparison.* However, in picking a date for surgery, one should consider the surgeon. A strong and positive doctor-patient relationship, as confirmed by a comparison of the charts, can minimize any negative influences on the date of surgery.

Unfortunately, most doctors and surgeons today do not have an accurate natal chart or are not willing to share this information with their patients. Perhaps if they did, the number of malpractice suits currently flooding our courts would be lessened. However, since we do not live in an ideal world, we must work with the available information. I always ask a doctor or dentist for their birth information after a few visits, and I encourage my readers to do so too. Perhaps one day our modern healers will take Hippocrates' statement seriously that only those with a knowledge of astrology can truly become expert at the healing arts.

If you can find out just your doctor's date of birth and if you have an accurately timed natal chart for yourself, you can still glean considerable understanding of the doctor-patient relationship. I am continually surprised at the ingenuity of my clients who by one means or another get this information. I found out a dentist's birthdate after a chance discussion with his dental hygienist, who noticed my astrological ring and asked if I was interested in astrology.

You don't have to be an expert in synastry to follow a few basic rules in selecting your medical healer, whether he or she is a doctor, dentist, chiropractor or nurse. In fact, these rules apply just as much to anyone whom you consult for help—a real-estate agent, lawyer, astrologer, theatrical or book agent, travel agent, banker, accountant or other person.

Before I outline the basic rules, let me anticipate one argument that is raised by some of our older and more traditional astrologers. There is a conflict of opinion as to whether doctors *et al* are under the symbolic rulership of Jupiter–Sagittarius–ninth house, where they are semi-deified as experts and only slightly lower than God, or of Venus–Libra–seventh house, where they are treated as peers who are consulted for their knowledge, not worshiped because of it. I think the public today is moving toward the second concept, and the medical profession, with perhaps a sigh of nostalgia for the good old days of the country doctor, is moving in this direction too. Thus in selecting a healer, you must give primary importance to your seventh house.

Specifically, you must pay close attention to the sign on the cusp of the seventh house, and select a doctor whose horoscope shows a strong emphasis of planets in that sign. Notice that I did not say one whose Sun is in that sign, although that would certainly be good, along with two or three other planets in that sign. However, the doctor's Sun in this sign is not a prerequisite. If his or her Ascendant is in the sign opposite the sign on your Ascendant (that is, in the sign on the cusp of your seventh house), that is also a beneficial indicator. A stellium in the doctor's chart corresponding to your seventh-house sign is also another very positive indicator. To find that your doctor's Jupiter by sign position falls either in your seventh house or closely conjunct your Sun's sign position would indeed be a very happy discovery.

If you already have a doctor or dentist whom you respect and admire, do not be surprised to discover a number of very positive cross-ties between your horoscopes. Even with no knowledge of astrology, many people almost instinctively select the right healer. A later chart comparison of the healer-patient relationship only serves to confirm what the patient knows intuitively.

In selecting your healer astrologically, there are also several negative indicators to be considered. Perhaps the strongest negative indicator would be the doctor's natal Saturn either conjunct or opposed to your natal Sun, keeping the orb to not more than ±5°. One interpretation of this cross combination is that the person whose Sun is contacted has a very valuable lesson to learn from the Saturn person. This may be true in many cases; however, the lesson might be to use more care in the future in selecting your doctor! In the extreme, such a relationship can turn into a master-slave relationship in which the patient blindly follows the doctor's directions with little or no understanding of the patient's role in the healing process. This is most often true under the conjunction; under the opposition the patient is often resistant, consciously or unconsciously, to the healer's instructions.

Another unfavorable indicator is a conjunction or opposition of the patient's Sun to the position of Neptune in the healer's chart. Under this aspect, the patient may feel a very strong attraction to the healer, sometimes almost to the point of worship. To a lesser extent, this is also true when the healer's Neptune is in similar aspect to the patient's Ascendant. Under such circumstances the patient often feels that he or she is receiving much more help than is actually the case, and ultimately the healer falls from the pedestal upon which the patient has placed him. At the present time, people with the Sun in Leo, Virgo or Libra and children with their Sun in Scorpio should pay particular attention to this point, as should those whose Ascendant is in these signs.

The art of synastry recognizes other negative indicators, but with most of them, such as Sun–Mars and Mars–Saturn contacts, the patient would not stay long with that healer because of antagonism that arises right away.

I might also mention several other significators that medical astrologers often feel should be avoided. While I do not consider them as important as those I have already mentioned, they probably should be avoided when possible. These negatives principally concern planets in the chart of the healer that by their sign position fall in your seventh house. Some astrologers I know refuse to consult with clients when Saturn in one chart falls in the seventh house of the other. Other astrologers interpret this to mean that the tie is karmic in nature and unavoidable. Under the rules of horary astrology, a seventh-house Saturn means that the horary chart is not to be read.

My personal observation has led me to conclude that it is best to avoid a healer whose Mars, Saturn or Neptune falls in the patient's seventh house. On the other hand, the healer's Jupiter, Sun or Venus in the patient's seventh house is a strongly positive indication. When the healer's Moon falls in the patient's seventh house, the outcome of the relationship is usually unpredictable—at one time beneficial, at another time seemingly of little help at all. Healers whose Saturn falls in the patient's third or twelfth house should also be avoided whenever possible.

In the ultimate analysis, if you can obtain an accurately timed birth chart of the healer, there is no substitute for a thorough analysis of this chart, both to understand the healer's basic personality and to compare it to the patient's chart. And although some people will contest this conclusion, everything I have said here applies equally to selecting a personal astrologer.

The Horary Chart

The value of a horary chart in selecting a date for surgery remains a controversial topic. One of the first problems is what data to use in constructing such a chart. Does one use the time when the patient is first informed that surgery is necessary, the time when the patient decides to go ahead with it, or the date and time of the operation? Does one use the latitude and longitude of the patient's residence or the coordinates of the place where the surgery is to be performed? These are hard questions to resolve, and among professionals there is little consensus.

In my own observation, a horary chart is of only second-ary value in determining a time for surgery. However, there is one important exception, which is of little help ahead of time, but which can be quite revealing after the fact. I have found that after the operation has been performed, an event chart drawn for the date, time and place of the operation can be revealing as to the outcome and length of recuperation.

In reading such an event chart, one applies the usual as-trological rules, paying particular attention to the condition of the Sun (vitality), the Moon (ambient environmental conditions) and Mars (the surgeon), along with hard aspects to these planets and the condition of the third, sixth, seventh and twelfth houses.

If the Sun and the twelfth house are favorable, the period for recovery is usually rapid and quite uneventful. Favorable third house conditions can contribute markedly to the patient's mental attitude and thus to the favorable outcome. An afflicted Mars, especially when squared or opposed by Pluto, is often an indicator of postoperative infection or bleeding and possibly excessive scarring. When Mars is squared or opposed by the Moon, swelling is often excessive. Finally, contrary to what I have been told by a number of my astrological colleagues, I find no evidence that a void-of-course Moon in an event chart means that the operation "comes to naught," although I continue to keep an open mind on this point.

While astrology can give us all some very remarkable in-sights into our problems and can help time events for maximum benefit, nevertheless we must work constantly to separate fact from fancy. We can learn much from our forebears, the magnifi-cent astrologers who have gone before us; however, there is no substitute for personal observation and conclusions based on events in our own life and in the lives of persons close to us. In this chapter I have outlined some of the general rules laid down by the ancient astrologers, colored by my own observations. To my knowledge, these rules are based upon empirical observation only and have never been fully tested in a statistical manner that would satisfy a scientist. If astrological research were funded as well as other scientific studies, perhaps the validity of these empirical observations could be more fully tested.

Without hard scientific proof for these rules, I most earnestly urge you, the reader, to test their validity in the light of your own experience. Some of these rules may be nothing more than old wives' tales based on the superstitions of the observers who first set down the rules. My own observations over the years tend to bear out these rules, but no astrologer is infallible, and all our observations are subject to revision based on new knowledge.

It is often not possible to pick an "ideal" date for some surgical procedure. In that case you should try to choose a date on which the astrological hazards of surgery are minimal. I would be the last to urge someone to postpone needed surgery because of less-than-ideal astrological conditions. On the other hand, if there is some leeway for the day, there seems to be little danger and great potential advantage in picking the date that seems most promising for success.

13

TIMES OF
BIRTH AND DEATH

It has been said that life is a terminal illness from which no one recovers. It has a distinct beginning and a distinct ending, both of which are very important to astrologers. But astrologers, doctors, philosophers, lawyers and the Church have found it very difficult to define precisely when life begins and when it ends. There is as yet no precise and widely accepted definition for either event. However, for a variety of reasons, all of these professions are being forced to define both birth and death in more precise terms. The current abortion controversy has certainly caused us all to ask: "When does life commence?" As long as astrology continues to place such a heavy emphasis on the natal chart, we too must meet this problem head on. Astrologers can no longer skirt this very important issue.

As an astrologer and a Scorpio, this matter of birth and death concerns me particularly, and I think it requires much more frank and open discussion in astrological textbooks. Such discussion certainly has a proper and important place in a book about health and nutrition, which is why I have chosen to discuss this topic in the final chapter.

The Time of Birth

Modern astrology has always insisted on the necessity of obtaining an "exact" birthtime in order to cast a correct natal horoscope. As professional astrologers, we tell our clients that the accuracy of our delineations depends on the accuracy of the birthtime provided by the client. Yet there is no consensus among astrologers as to exactly what this time is.

In most cases we rely on the time recorded on some official document (usually a birth certificate), in a baby book or in the family Bible. Then, by a variety of methods, we attempt to refine or rectify this time by a few minutes one way or another to make it more accurate. Often the official recorded birthtime is off by a considerable margin. The introduction of Daylight Saving Time has complicated this problem even more. For a number of years, Illinois and Pennsylvania had laws that required all birthtimes to be recorded in Standard Time, whether or not Daylight Saving Time or War Time were in effect. However, many doctors failed to do this. So people born in those states can never be certain whether the time on their birth certificates is Daylight Saving Time or Standard Time. For those born in New Jersey during Daylight Saving Time, the situation is even worse. Having no legislation on the matter, the state assumes that all times are reported as Standard Time.

I shall not belabor this discussion with all of the other variables that further confuse this important moment, such as states like Indiana that have switched time zones frequently with little record of the years when the changes were made. The point is: there is a great deal of confusion about official birthtimes.

This matter is complicated still further by the variety of definitions of birthtime currently in use. Perhaps the most widely held definition is that birthtime is the moment when the newborn babe takes its first breath. In Oriental philosophy this is considered the moment when the soul enters the physical body. Some people hold that the birth moment is when the baby commences life independent of the mother, usually symbolized by the severance of the umbilical cord.

There is also an interesting new school of thought, supported by some new findings in biochemistry, that the birthtime is the moment when the crown of the head emerges from the mother. More precisely, it is the moment when light first strikes the top of the head, since light is thought to trigger a whole series of reactions in the pineal body that prepare the baby for independent existence (see Chapter Eight). The problem with this theory is that so little is known about the pineal body.

Accuracy and Precision

To anyone with scientific training, measurement is of paramount importance. The scientist looks at the astrologer and asks: "What are you measuring when you cast a natal chart?" Even more important is the question: "For what purpose is the measurement being taken?" If we as astrologers claim that the natal horoscope is a symbolic picture of a person's basic makeup and personality, then we had better come to some determination of what it is that we are really measuring and, even more important, how precise and accurate this measurement must be. Unfortunately, most astrologers do not understand what the terms "accurate" and "precise" mean to the scientist.

Perhaps I can explain this problem more simply with an example. Suppose we wish to find out the area of a floor. If our reason for doing this is to find out the total square footage of the house, then the length and width measurements accurate to the nearest inch give us all the information we need. But if our purpose is to measure the floor for linoleum, the measurements should be accurate to the nearest quarter inch. In this case we would probably check our measurements several times to see if they are precise. If they check out to within an eighth of an inch each time, we can say that they are precise to an eighth of an inch. But if the ruler is off by a half inch, our measurements would still be precise to an eighth of an inch, but they would not be accurate.

Modern computers are able to give us very precise calculations, and many astrologers now use computers routinely to cast a natal chart. However, the accuracy of the chart is based on the birthtime provided. If this time is correct, the chart is both precise and accurate; if the birthtime is incorrect, then the chart, although precise, is inaccurate.

This raises several questions. First, do we need this kind of computer precision in calculating a horoscope, when we have no clear-cut definition of what constitutes the moment of birth? Second, we must ask what we are attempting to measure. Is it absolutely essential that the position of every planet and every house cusp in the horoscope be calculated to the nearest minute of a degree? Or, to put it another way, would your delineation of the chart change materially if the Ascendant or the Sun were off by as much as one degree? Some charts are very time sensitive, and in such cases an error of this magnitude might place some planet or cusp in a different sign. But even in this case, we must ask ourselves—based on experience, primarily—if the change is that significant in the overall delineation.

When we state that a planet in the horoscope is at 10° of Cancer, we imply that we have measured its position to an accuracy of ±1°. If, however, we state that the planet is at 10° Cancer 38', we imply a much greater degree of accuracy, of 1 minute of one degree. In this case, is knowing the planet's position to the nearest minute of a degree important? Would this accuracy materially change your delineation, or is 10° of Cancer sufficient for the purpose?

From the scientist's point of view, presenting a natal chart of such great accuracy to a client implies great accuracy of interpretation as well. But we all know that each astrologer delineates a horoscope from his or her own unique point of view. Obviously, if chart delineations were precise, any three astrologers would interpret a natal chart in exactly the same way. The accuracy of the delineation depends, of course, on the astrologer's learning, knowledge and experience.

This problem is not unique to astrology; many other professions suffer from the same problem. In psychology, for example, does an IQ of 130 really mean that a person is smarter than someone with an IQ of 125? In medicine, would a doctor's diagnosis be very different if a blood sugar level were 110 mg. instead of 100 mg.? We must ask ourselves if the precision and accuracy of the measurements are not a kind of overkill? How precise and accurate must our measurements be in order to solve the problem and do our job well? Is knowing the birthtime within five minutes sufficient in helping the client? Ten minutes? Twenty? Half a minute? This question has not been settled, although we'd all like to have the greatest accuracy possible. But do we need it in order to do a workmanlike job of delineation? That is a question that each astrologer must decide for himself. In measuring our astrological room, is it necessary to know all of the dimensions to within a quarter inch, or is it sufficient to describe the room as being "less than a city block in length but longer than a breadbox"?

Unlike chemistry or physics, astrology is not a precise science, nor do I think it ever will be, as long as the human mind, with all its variables, is a part of the total equation. The calculation of the chart may be done scientifically, based on accurate observations of the planetary positions, but the interpretation must always remain an art, based on the skill and knowledge of the interpreter. Astrology is not, therefore, a science like chemistry but an art/science, and it is important for us to recognize the difference.

The Time of Death

The problem of the moment of death is just as complicated for society as the moment of birth. When does the body die? When the heart stops beating? When the intelligence ceases to function and the nerve cells of the brain die? Is it murder to stop artificial life-support systems when the heart continues to beat after the brain cells have died?

Some American astrologers have recently posed a very interesting question. In the case of cardiac arrest, in which the heart stops beating momentarily and is started again through medical procedures, does the natal horoscope change? Should a new horoscope be drawn for the individual based on the moment when the heartbeat is restored?

Every professional astrologer has had clients inquiring

about death. "My mother is ill. Will she die?" "Will I have a long life?" "Will I recover from my illness?" Evangeline Adams has said that in any given year of a person's life there are several occasions when an astrologer might prophesy death, because of certain progressions, eclipses or transits. Some argue that our Creator, in whatever form we conceive of this entity, meant for us to discover the purpose of our lives through astrology but did not mean for us to know the time or conditions of death. Passages from the Bible certainly tend to confirm this view. For ethical reasons, most astrologers will not discuss this topic with a client except in the most general terms, because they recognize that astrology has not yet advanced to the point of being able to answer this question. Occasional claims to the contrary by certain astrologers do more to injure than to help astrology in my view, especially predictions of assassination of prominent people.

However, hindsight is always more accurate than foresight, so I do not think that ethical considerations should stop astrological researchers from comparing a person's natal chart with the progressions and transits at the time of death as reported in official records. Much can be learned from such comparisons.

In the rest of this chapter we shall examine the current knowledge of death as revealed using the horoscope. Although this knowledge must be considered incomplete, we can all profit from what has been observed. We shall examine the birth and death charts of President Lyndon B. Johnson, using the officially recorded time of his death.

HOUSE IMPLICATIONS. Traditionally, astrologers associate death and related matters with the eighth house in the horoscope. Most astrological texts describe this house as symbolizing all matters regarding death, especially inheritance and legacy. It is the natural house of Scorpio and of Pluto, to which most astrologers ascribe death matters.

The fourth house is also important, because it symbolizes not only retirement and one's last years, but also the disposition of one's mortal remains. I believe that the fourth house also contributes to our understanding of the cause and condition of death from the broader perspective of medical astrology.

PLANETARY IMPLICATIONS.   Pluto is often referred to as the alpha and omega, the beginning and the ending. It represents both the moment of creation, the fusion of sperm and egg in a "hidden place," and the moment of death. Pluto's house location can sometimes be very revealing. Pluto in the tenth, for example, usually means that the person's death will be a matter of public record or importance.

Saturn represents "Father Time." It represents where we are karmically when we choose to be born (and we do choose our parents) and where we "ought" to be when we finally die. It is life's stopwatch: click, and life starts; click again, and life ends. Saturn in the eighth house delays death, or in other words, it prolongs life. Jupiter in the first house or Sagittarius rising is said to signal a long life. Statistics indicate that those with Sagittarius rising tend to live longer than people with other rising signs. And Jupiter or Venus in the fourth house indicate not only pleasant retirement years but also a painless or happy death.

SIGN IMPLICATIONS.   The sign on the cusp of the fourth or the eighth house is generally related to the anatomical region or physiological process that is directly implicated in the cause of death. Planets in these signs or houses are also very important. Uranus in the fourth or eighth house or Aries or Aquarius on their cusps, for example, in some cases indicates violent death or death as the result of an accident. Mars rules automobiles, and car accidents are sometimes related to Mars in the fourth or the eighth. Electrocution, ruled by Uranus, is sometimes related to Uranus in the fourth or the eighth. The sign Cancer on the cusp of the fourth or eighth, according to Cornell, is related to death by cancer, and Pluto (growths or tumors) is frequently implicated. Leo and/or the Sun are frequently related to death from heart failure or heart attack; Aries, to head injuries or stroke; Gemini, to respiratory disease; Virgo and Pisces, to bacterial disease.

173

Longevity and the Hyleg

The traditional method for judging longevity is by studying the Hyleg planet, which is said to be the prorogator or giver of life, and the aspects to this planet. Malefic aspects to the Hyleg planet by transit or progression are said to be very important in understanding the cause of death. Selection of the Hyleg planet is one of the most controversial topics in medical astrology. There are many complicated systems for determining this planet, complicated even further by the different house systems. Endless hours of study have led me to the following simplified system for understanding this complex matter. As I will shortly demonstrate, you must have an accurate birth chart; a solar chart cannot be used, because it always makes the Sun the Hyleg planet for a male. The house system can be very important in making this determination; I continue to use the Placidean system, although the Koch system also shows promise.

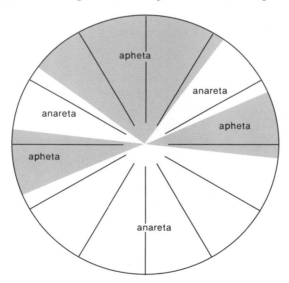

Figure 4. The aphetic regions of the horoscope.

174

In all discussions of longevity, we speak of the Apheta, the giver of life, and the Anareta, its taker. The Aphetic places in the chart extend from the 25th degree of the eighth house to the 25th degree of the eleventh house; from the 25th degree of the twelfth house to the 25th degree of the first house; and from the 25th degree of the sixth house to the 25th degree of the seventh house. The remaining areas of the chart are Anaretic regions.

In the chart of a male, the Sun is the Hyleg planet if it is located in one of the Aphetic regions shown above. If the Sun is not in an Aphetic region, use Jupiter or the Moon, if they are Aphetic, selecting the one that is best aspected. In the chart of a female, the Moon is Hyleg if located in an Aphetic region; if the Moon is not Aphetic, use Venus if it is Aphetic; otherwise, the Ascendant is Hyleg.

The degree of the Ascendant rising at birth is always very important and, according to Cornell, is usually afflicted and badly involved in death. He further points out that Aphetic planets in the chart in good aspect to the Hyleg tend to prolong life, while Anaretic planets, especially Saturn and Mars if Anaretic, tend to shorten it. Saturn afflicting the Hyleg is said to indicate death through some disease, while Mars afflicting the Hyleg is often involved in violent death. Transits and progressions of Mars and Saturn over the Hyleg are said to weaken the vitality while within an orb of 1° of the Hyleg.

Before we turn to an example of these indications of death, I should remind you of this most important rule: *It takes three or more indicators in the chart to show death or the possibility of death.*

The Death of President Johnson

Lyndon B. Johnson was born August 27, 1908, at 4:18 A.M., LMT at 98° W 25' and 30° N 16'. He died of a heart attack shortly after 3:30 P.M. on January 22, 1973, at the LBJ Ranch, not far from his place of birth. The heart attack, in which the blood flow to the coronary arteries is blocked, resulted from what doctors call congestive heart failure. He had experienced earlier severe heart attacks in mid-1955, when he was forty-six, and in April, 1972, which left him subject to recurrent and violent attacks of angina pectoris, severe chest pains. He was overweight and had arteriosclerosis, the accumulation of fatty material in the coronary arteries. The overworked heart muscle vented its complaint as angina. Because the left ventricle of the heart, the main pumping chamber, could not do its work efficiently, it began to enlarge. The resulting high blood pressure interfered with the kidneys' eliminative function, and the body retained too much fluid, which is all part of the process called congestive heart failure.

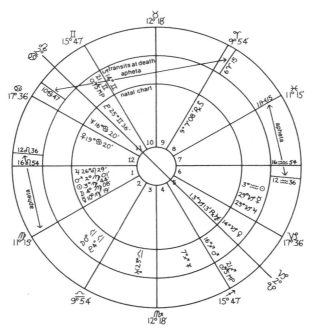

Figure 5. Johnson's natal chart, transits at death and aphetic regions

Now let us see what information about this condition we can derive from his natal and death charts. To begin with, according to the above rules for determining the Hyleg planet, the Sun is Hyleg in Johnson's chart, giving him plenty of vitality and resistance to disease, in his first house. This fact alone may account for the fact that he was able to survive the first two massive heart attacks. Notice next that only Neptune, Venus and Uranus are Anareta in his chart. Thus we have our first clue: to look for these three planets to be deeply involved in his death.

Capricorn-Saturn rules his sixth (health) house, indicating that restriction of some type was his major health problem. Cancer-Moon rules his twelfth house, indicating a potentially chronic problem related to the body fluids. Venus in the twelfth would tend to keep him out of hospitals, but because Venus is Anareta and semisquare his Sun, sweets and overweight contributed to his ill health. He smoked two or three packs of cigarettes a day, which certainly added to his health problems. Neptune, symbolizing nicotine, is conjunct Venus, semisquare the Sun and ruler of the eighth house. Neptune is Anareta. The fifth house, the natural house of Leo rules the heart. The fifth is ruled by Jupiter-Sagittarius. Jupiter represents the arterial blood circulation, and Uranus in the fifth can indicate sudden seizures. Uranus too is Anareta.

Turning now to his death chart, we find that all of the planets by transit, except Saturn, are Anareta, which means that at the time of his death they were unable to give him any protection. Life is protected only by major aspects to the Hyleg from planets that are Apheta. Saturn (Apheta) could do little more from its position in Gemini than make his death less painful (sextile his Leo Ascendant) and very much a matter of public notice (tenth house).

Now we come to a very important point—the matter of quincunxes (150° aspect) in the death chart. There are usually several quincunxes between natal points and transiting planets at the time of death. Johnson's chart shows three extremely important transiting quincunx aspects: Sun quincunx natal Sun. Venus quincunx the Leo Ascendant from the fifth house, where it is also conjunct natal. Uranus, and Saturn quincunx natal Uranus and transiting Venus. Saturn's transiting placement at his death completes the Saturn–Ascendant–Uranus Yod. I believe that this Yod in great measure explains why he survived his two previous heart attacks and not this one—because the Yod did not exist in the earlier ones. The Yod is said to represent the hand of fate.

Johnson's vitality just before his death was about as low as it could get. Transits of the Sun through the sixth house each year always bring on a period of lowered vitality, the low point in this case being an exact quincunx of natal and transiting Sun.

We pointed out that Venus, Neptune and Uranus were natally Anareta, so what were they doing in Johnson's chart at death? Transiting Venus was conjunct natal Uranus; transiting Neptune was square the natal Sun (remember, Neptune rules the eighth house of death) and in close trine to Saturn in the eighth.

Of more than passing interest is the fact that Pluto (significator of death) in Gemini is at the Mars-Saturn midpoint (21° Gemini/Sagittarius) natally, which is the focus of inhibited or destroyed vitality in the chart, according to Ebertin. Mars by transit (physical energy) is almost at that point and has just entered the fifth house. The heart is a muscle, and Mars rules muscles in general.

The Moon's position by transit is generally important in some way at the exact time of death. And at Johnson's death the Moon was right on the Virgo/Libra cusp. At almost his exact moment of death, it was leaving Virgo, the sign that his Moon is in natally, to form a conjunction with Pluto by transit. Moon–Pluto conjunctions often signal the death of an important person or a national leader.

According to *Time* magazine, "He ate a leisurely lunch at the LBJ Ranch . . . and then donned his pajamas for an afternoon nap. Shortly after 3:30 P.M., stricken, he snatched up his bedroom phone and gasped out one last order: send Mike (his Secret Service guard) immediately. They found him crumpled on the bedroom floor, his face blue from lack of oxygen. [Remember restricting Saturn in Gemini, the lungs.] Mouth-to-mouth resuscitation failed. They carried him to his private plane at the ranch landing strip, but by the time the plane reached San Antonio a quarter of an hour later, they knew that he was dead."

Jupiter, which rules the general circulation and in particular the arterial circulation, is close to Johnson's Ascendant. Natal and transiting Jupiter are also quincunx and natally in Leo, his "heart" circulation. Generally, under quincunx, attempts to do something fail, here the attempts to restore his circulation and make the heart pump again.

Jupiter is also opposed to Johnson's Point of Death (the Ascendant plus the cusp of the eighth house), which is the Moon, 24° 01' Aquarius. Those who use these Arabian points generally work only with tight conjunctions or oppositions. Here the orb is 2° 28'. The Point of Death is in the seventh house, which indicates that he would probably not die unattended but have someone at his side, in this case his Secret Service agent. Are you surprised then to learn that the seventh house does represent agents?

Other points in Johnson's natal and death charts might be mentioned as additional evidence that astrology does explain much about death. There are surely many more than three indicators of death here. The evidence is almost overwhelming, and yet I feel that it would have been difficult to predict this death beforehand. In any study of death charts, hindsight is always better than foresight, although the three planets Anareta and the Hyleg certainly foreshadow events to come.

In pondering this example, you might ask yourself: "Would knowing all this beforehand have been of any value to President Johnson?" I subscribe to the astrological ethic that the astrologer should never predict the date or time of death for any client, even when it seems certain. I believe that our death is written in the stars, just like every other important event in our lives. Furthermore, I believe that comparing natal and death charts of individuals whose lives are known is a fruitful field of astrological research. It has certainly fascinated me, but I am a

Scorpio, and as they get older, Scorpios are said to be more and more preoccupied with matters related to death and the meaning of life.

Earlier I pointed out that the fourth house indicates the place of burial. Scorpio-Pluto rules Johnson's fourth house. Scorpio is a water sign, and Pluto indicates lonely, out-of-the-way places. And where was he buried? At his own request, in a lonely cow pasture close to the slow-moving river that flows through his ranch. Neptune by transit occupied his fourth house at the time of death. As ruler of the twelfth house, Neptune rules large animals, such as cattle. After leaving the White House, Johnson raised cattle on his ranch. Certainly, Neptune was here all during that time. Pluto rules the fourth house, so he will be remembered for a long time after his death.

In President Johnson's nodal chart, there is a heavy planetary emphasis in houses four and nine. As discussed in Chapter Eleven, these houses in the nodal chart govern the lower abdominal area, including the kidneys, which eliminate fluid wastes from the body. Johnson's Saturn in the nodal fourth indicates potential problems in the lower abdomen, caused by some organ not functioning up to capacity. If the kidneys do not function properly, fluids may accumulate in the body; fluid build-up is a major contributing factor in congestive heart failure, which was the cause of Johnson's death. According to his nodal chart, I would guess that his right kidney, represented by the fourth house, was the one that functioned least efficiently. Libra, which is on the Midheaven of Johnson's nodal chart, also governs the kidneys, and it rules the tenth house, which is most closely associated with the heart.

At the time of his death, the Moon, representing fluids, and Pluto, representing death, were in conjunction by transit, at 0° and 4°, respectively, of Libra. This conjunction was bracketing his nodal Midheaven, another indication of a major health problem with his heart, which led to his death.

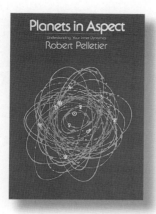

Planets in Aspect
Understanding Your Inner Dynamics.

Robert Pelletier.

Every major aspect (conjunction, sextile, square, trine, opposition, inconjunct) is covered, 314 aspects in all, 300 words per aspect, thumb indexed for easy reference. *Planets in Aspect,* the first volume published in Para Research's Planets series, is undoubtedly the most thorough in-depth study of planetary aspects (including the inconjuncts) ever written. It's intelligent, yet easy to read. It's personal, yet objective. It's astrology that really works... and keeps on working for you.

Planets in Composite
Analyzing Human Relationships.

Robert Hand

Planets in Composite contains an explanation of the composite technique, chapters on casting and reading the horoscope, five case studies illustrating the use and validity of composite charts, plus twelve chapters of delineations. There are delineations for all the planets (including Sun and Moon) in each house and every major aspect (conjunction, sextile, square, trine, opposition). 374 interpretations in all, 300 words each, thumb-indexed for easy reference. And there are 41 delineations of the Moon's nodes as well.

Size: 6 1/2" x 9 1/4" • • 363 pp.
ISBN: 978-0-914918-20-2 • soft • $19.99

Size: 6 1/2" x 9 1/4" • • 372 pp.
ISBN: 978-0-914918-22-6 • soft • $19.99

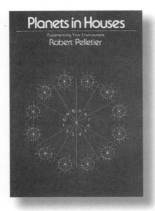

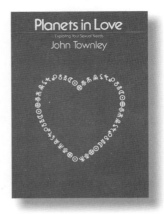

Planets in Houses
Experiencing Your Environment

Robert Pelletier

What Robert Pelletier does in *Planets in Houses* has never been done before in the history of astrology. He discusses the meaning of each planet in each house as derived by counting from each of the other eleven houses, and he discusses the meaning of each house position in relation to the other houses with which it forms trines, sextiles, squares and oppositions, inconjuncts and semi-sextiles.

In each chapter, wheel symbols graphically show the seventeen different house relationships delineated for each planet. Finally, Pelletier delineates the Sun-Moon polarities in terms of the wheel of houses: for each house position of the Sun, he interprets each of the twelve possible related house positions of the Moon. Each chapter presents the traditional meaning of the house and explains how the derivative house system applies to it.

Planets in Love
Exploring Your Emotional and Sexual Needs

John Townley

Planets in Love is the first astrology book to take an unabashed look at human sexuality and the variety of relationships people form to meet emotional sexual needs. With unusual depth and insight, author John Townley delineates each traditional horoscope factor in terms of love and sex.

Planets in Love contains a 300-word delineation of every planet and the Ascendant in every sign, every planet in every major house and planetary aspect. In all, there are 550 delineations written in terms of your sexual behavior and relationships.

This book provides a catalyst for couples to open up their communication about sexual and emotional issues. Moreover, it gives you a valuable guide for an ongoing process of discovery and exploration.

Size: 6 1/2" x 9 1/4" • • 372 pp.
ISBN: 0-914918-27-3 • soft • $24.95

Size: 6 1/2" x 9 1/4" • • 372 pp.
ISBN: 0-914918-21-4 • soft • $19.95

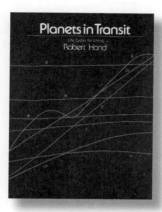

Planets in Transit
Life Cycles for Living. 2nd-revised.

Robert Hand

This book covers complete delineations
of all the major transits - conjunction,
sextile, square, trine and opposition - that
occur between transiting Sun, Moon and
all planets to each planet in the natal
chart and the Ascendant and Midheaven,
as well as complete delineations of each
planet transiting each house of the natal
chart. These 720 lucid delineations are
full of insight for both the professional
astrologer and the beginner.

Planets in Youth
Patterns of Early Development

Robert Hand

To Robert Hand, children are adults in
the process of becoming. Parents will
welcome this book and use it to help
their children learn to cope with the
complexities of modern life. Readers of all
ages will use it to understand their own
patterns of early development.

The first four chapters define the roles
of mother and father, explain the effects
of various planetary energy systems and
discuss the meaning of elements and
crosses in a child's chart. Hand analyzes
the charts of three children, including
Judy Garland and Shirley Temple, to
illustrate the astrological principles
and psychological insights set forth
in his intriguing study of personality
development.

The major part of the book consists of
delineations of horoscope factors, written
with young people in mind. Every planet
in every sign, house and major aspect, as
well as every rising sign, is interpreted
in about three hundred words that stress
possibilities rather than certainties.

Size: 6 1/2″ x 9 1/4″ • • 532 pp.
ISBN: 978-0-924608-26-1 • soft • $29.99

Size: 6 1/2″ x 9 1/4″ • • 372 pp.
ISBN: 0-914918-26-5 • soft • $24.95